Readers, whether pastors or not, will be strengthened, inspired, and encouraged by these truly biblical messages. I have no doubt that many of us will go repeatedly to these sermons for a fresh look at Jesus' parables and their application to the modern world — and especially to the modern church. Those who have ears to hear let them hear.

Lee McGlone: Ph.D. Retired Pastor, First Baptist Church, Arkadelphia, Arkansas; Interim Pastor, Calvary Baptist Church, Little Rock, Arkansas.
Adjunct Professor, Ouachita Baptist University, Arkadelphia, Arkansas.

Bill Tuck has done it again. He has brought his extensive pastoral experience, his real-world touch and his considerable academic background to bear. You will find usable materials here.

Peter Rhea Jones: J Truett Gannon Professor Emeritus of Preaching and New Testament, Mercer University McAfee School of Theology, and author of *Studying the Parables of Jesus*.

STORIES THAT CONTINUE TO SPEAK TO US TODAY

Looking Again At The Parables Of Jesus

William Powell Tuck is a prolific author and editor, previously publishing 36 titles for numerous publishers. In addition to *Stories That Continue to Speak To Us Today: Looking Again at the Parables of Jesus*, Tuck has published through CSS Publishing Company, Inc.:

Christmas is for the Young... Whatever Their Age

The Abiding Presence

Many of Tuck's titles can be found on Amazon.com.

Bill Tuck likes stories; short stories and long, all kinds of stories. That's what makes this book so special! Basically, it's about the stories of Jesus, which are so important in themselves. But Bill talks about them in the context of other stories, so that the stories and parts of stories all come alive for us. Preachers will love this book, because they'll want to tell the stories that Bill told. So will other readers. We all love stories, because they tell us about life and how to live it. And that's what makes this book a "must read."

John Killinger: former pastor and professor at Vanderbilt, Chicago, Princeton and Sanford University, and author of many books including *God, the Devil & Harry Potter*, and *Fundamentals of Preaching*.

There are so many books of sermons on the parables. I have almost twenty just on my shelf! Could preachers and laypeople need another one? The answer is "Yes" when it is William P. Tuck's *Stories that Continue to Speak to Us Today: Looking Again at the Parables of Jesus*. The author looks at seventeen parables through detailed biblical study, careful theological reflection, insightful hermeneutical consideration, and creative and engaging homiletical formulation. Several of the sermon titles reveal the penetrating quality of the book: "When Going to Church Doesn't Mean Much," "Emptiness Invites Unwanted Guests," "The End of Privilege and the Invitation to Unlikely Guests," "A Reason for Living," "Squirming in the Net of Judgement." With imaginative language, crisp turns of phrase, illustrations that are just right, the preacher brings these stories alive in such a way that they speak to us today. This book would be ideal background for sermons — including sermon series — and it would be an excellent resource for Bible study class or group as well as for individual reading.

Ronald J. Allen: Professor of Preaching and Gospels and Letters Christian Theological Seminary, Indianapolis.

Since Jesus proclaimed so much of his message in parables, those who dare to preach and teach in his name must endeavor to interpret these short stories for the people of God today. But that is easier said than done! Though drawn from simple, everyday scenarios, Jesus' parables are no little moralistic tales. They pack a dizzying punch, challenging every aspect of our lives. We need a faithful, insightful guide to light our way, and Bill Tuck fits that bill perfectly. As a seasoned professor and pastor, Tuck has wrestled long and hard with these parables. In this volume, he shares the fruit of his study and preaching in clear and vibrant language, fully engaged with the Gospel texts and contemporary Christian life. Highly recommended for ministers, students, and laypersons alike.

F. Scott Spencer: Professor of New Testament and Biblical Interpretation at Baptist Theological Seminary at Richmond.

Dr. Bill Tuck has once again produced a helpful volume for pastors, students of preaching, as well as parishioners who seek a positive model for interpreting and applying biblical insight. Here Dr. Tuck opens our hearts and minds to the powerful images from Jesus' parables.

The introductory article, "Preaching on the Parables," is insightful, delightful, challenging, and worthy of a close reading. The seventeen sermons that follow are marked by attention to eternal truth, the essential "kernel" that rises from within the parable and guides the sermon as it progresses. Evident also are numerous examples of Dr. Tuck's interpretive insights regarding the elements of "surprise" and also "humor." Illustrations are abundant and tastefully chosen from scripture, history, literature, current events, and personal stories that add warmth and life.

STORIES THAT CONTINUE TO SPEAK TO US TODAY

Looking Again At The Parables Of Jesus

Willam Powell Tuck

CSS Publishing Company, Inc.
Lima, Ohio

STORIES THAT CONTINUE TO SPEAK TO US

FIRST EDITION
Copyright © 2022
by CSS Publishing Co., Inc.

The original purchaser may print and photocopy material in this publication for use as it was intended (worship material for worship use; educational material for classroom use; dramatic material for staging or production). No additional permission is required from the publisher for such copying by the original purchaser only. Inquiries should be addressed to: Permissions, CSS Publishing Company, Inc., 5450 N. Dixie Highway, Lima, Ohio 45807.

Library of Congress Cataloging-in-Publication Data

Names: Tuck, William Powell, 1934- author.
Title: Stories that continue to speak to us today : looking again at the parables of Jesus / William Powell Tuck.
Description: First edition. | Lima, Ohio : CSS Publishing Company, Inc., 2022.
Identifiers: LCCN 2021046069 | ISBN 9780788030628 (paperback) | ISBN 9780788030635 (ebook)
Subjects: LCSH: Jesus Christ--Parables.
Classification: LCC BT375.3 .T83 2022 | DDC 226.8/06--dc23/eng/20211130
LC record available at https://lccn.loc.gov/2021046069

For more information about CSS Publishing Company resources, visit our website at www.csspub.com, email us at csr@csspub.com, or call (800) 241-4056.

e-book:
ISBN-13: 978-0-7880-3063-5
ISBN-10: 0-7880-3063-9

ISBN-13: 978-0-7880-3062-8
ISBN-10: 0-7880-3062-0

For Emily,
My loving companion on life's journey
and
wonderful teacher and storyteller

CONTENTS

Preface	13
Preaching On The Parables	15
Lessons From A Dishonest Man (Parable of the Dishonest Manager) Luke 16: 1-13	20
Big Shots In The Church (Parable of the Cheap Seats) Luke 14: 7-11	32
When Going To Church Doesn't Mean Much (Parable of the Pharisee and the Publican) Luke 18: 9-14	45
Trying To Make A Patch Do (Parable of a New Patch on an Old Garment) Luke 5: 36-39	56
The End Of Privilege And The Invitation To Unlikely Guests (Parable of the Great Feast) Luke 14: 7-24	66
Work: A Gift Of Trust (Parable of the Talents) Matthew 25: 14-30	77
Standing Up For Kindness (Parable of the Good Samaritan) Luke 10: 25-37	86
Emptiness Invites Unwanted Guests (Parable of the Haunted House) Matthew 12: 43-45	98
Finding Forgiveness (Parable of the Prodigal Son) Luke 15: 11-32	107
On Being Ready (Parable of the Wise and Foolish Bridesmaids) Matthew 25: 1-13	118

A Reason For Living — 129
(Parable of the Barren Fig Tree)
Luke 13: 6-9

Making Your Future — 136
(Parable of the Tenants in the Vineyard)
Mark 12: 1-12

A Triumphant Note Of Joy — 145
(Parables of the Lost Sheep and the Lost Coin)
Luke 15: 3-10

Building For The Long Haul — 155
(Parable of the Rock Foundation)
Luke 6: 46-49

How Do You Listen? — 164
(Parable of the Four Soils)
Matthew 13: 3-9; 18-23

Does It Do Any Good To Pray? — 175
(Parable of the Friend Coming at Midnight)
Luke 11: 5-13

Squirming In The Net Of Judgment — 186
(Parable of the Dragnet)
Matthew 13: 47-48

Preface

I have always loved stories; hearing them and reading them as a child, reading short stories, plays, and novels as a young person as well as an adult. My wife Emily is a marvelous story teller, whether it is a family story or one she shares from her reading. We all love to hear her tell a story in her exceptional way. Stories capture our attention and imagination and linger in our mind long after the hearing or reading of them. Parishioners tell me they remember the stories or illustrations from my sermons when they can recall nothing else. I know that is also true from my listening to the sermons of other preachers. I think that's the reason Henry Mitchell in his Lyman Beecher Lectures, *The Recovery of Preaching*, warns the preacher: "If you have an idea that can't be translated into a story or a picture, don't tell it."[1] Listeners, whether in church or in a classroom or some other place, remember stories.

I think Jesus knew this well, and that's the reason he told stories or parables, as the gospels refer to them. Oh, I know, some New Testament scholars claim Jesus used parables to hide his deeper or "mysterious" meaning of his teaching. But that makes no sense to me. I believe he used them because he knew people would remember them, even when the deeper meaning might be obscured and needed explanation from him. On several occasions, his disciples would ask him to clarify the meaning of a parable. But his listeners remembered them. Do not misunderstand. I am not implying that Jesus' parables are like sermon illustrations today. His parables challenged the listeners to use their imagination to envision the spiritual meaning he was projecting. Often his parabolic form veiled an obvious meaning to reveal a deeper spiritual insight that addressed his listeners in a startling or unexpected way. Peter Rhea Jones, in his book, *Studying the Parables of Jesus*, also reminds us that Jesus not only told parables but engaged in "parabolic acts" like cleansing the temple, cursing a fig tree, receiving outcasts, riding into Jerusalem on Palm Sunday on a donkey, washing the disciples' feet with a towel and basin, and the redefining of bread and wine at the Last Supper.[2] Scholars offer different readings on the number of parables Jesus taught. Among scholars, A. B. Bruce suggested 33 with 8 as "parable germs;" Richard C. Trench 53; A. M. Hunter 60; Joachim Jeremias 60; George Buttrick 44, William Barclay 33, and Bernard Brandon Scott treats 33, as well. The number varies because some claim parabolic sayings in their listings.

Throughout my years of ministry, preaching the parables of Jesus has been one of my great pleasures in proclaiming the good news from and about Jesus. I have over fifty books on the parables by scholars and preachers in my personal library, not counting my dozens of commentaries, which have provided me excellent resources on the parables of Jesus. I have preached some on selected Sundays and others in several series of sermons on the parables. I have selected several sermons from my preaching through the years for this book. Several others are included in the sermon collection *The Forgotten Beatitude: Worshiping through Stewardship.*[3] I have had the pleasure of teaching courses on the parables at pastors' conferences and seminars, in churches, seminary classes, and at the "Bible-Preaching Conference" at the Ridgecrest Baptist Center in North Carolina on one occasion. I have included some brief suggestions for preaching on the parables in another section. I want to express my appreciation again to my friend and fellow minister, Rand Forder, for his reading my manuscript in an early stage. He is always helpful and gracious in giving his time and attention to this matter.

Preaching On The Parables

Although ministers have preached on the parables of Jesus for hundreds of years, it is probably harder to do so today than it has ever been. Many of the parables are taken from rural or agricultural settings and may not seem to have a proper role in a scientific and urban age. Others dismiss them as childish or "Sunday school" stories, unworthy of serious study by modern men and women. Nevertheless, some New Testament scholars see the renewed interest in the parables as one of most important biblical happenings in the past fifty years. Other than the Beatitudes and the Lord's Prayer, the parables are among the best known and loved of the teachings of Jesus. The parables comprise more than a third of the teachings of Jesus. Scholars differ on the number of parables in the gospels. Some list as many as seventy; while others list only thirty. A child was asked one day what was her favorite part of the Bible. "The like sayings," she answered. Many of us would agree.

Parables were a familiar Jewish method of teaching. Numerous parables can be found in the Old Testament. Note especially 2 Samuel 12:1-4, 2 Kings 14:9, Isaiah 5:1-6, 28: 23-29, Jeremiah 1;11-13, 13:1-11, 13:12-14, 18:1-13, 19: 1-5, 24:1-10, and many others. How do we define a parable? A little girl said: "A parable is an earthly story with a heavenly meaning." That's not bad. A parable is a picture image or narrative drawn from a familiar realm, such as nature or domestic life, to convey a spiritual truth. A parable may be a metaphor, simile, word picture or a story designed to illuminate a spiritual truth about life. Jesus drew his parables from the home, farm, city streets, fields, weddings, children playing, baking, sewing, the market place, and from the ordinary places of life. The parable may begin in such a way that the listener feels that the speaker is addressing someone else and he or she is at a safe distance, but before one realizes it, unexpectedly, he or she is drawn into the story and the pointer is directed their way. Rather than seeing the parables as simple stories with obvious moral teachings, readers and listeners have been invited to enter a picture gallery and see themselves in the mirrors within and respond to the personal summons that each solicits from its participants.

Preparing To Preach On Parables

Someone has said that the saxophone is a musical instrument that is easy to play poorly. The same can be said for preaching on parables. Often preachers think a parable has an obvious meaning and requires no study, research or preparation before one preaches on it. That is a mistake. Let me offer ten suggestions for the preacher to consider as he or she prepares to preach on the parables.

1. Before one preaches on a parable, careful study needs to be done on the context of the parable in the text; what is the central theme of the parable, and what was its intent by Jesus? The background and circumstances surrounding the telling of a particular parable are essential to knowing its meaning.

2. Remember that a parable is not an allegory and one should not try to find fantastic meanings in the images or characters in the parables. This was the method often used by such people in the first several centuries of Christianity like Marcion, Irenaeus, Tertullian, Origen, and even Augustine. The one parable that may be an exception to this rule and have some allegorical features is the one on "The Wicked Tenants" in Mark 12: 1-12.

3. Simply making a running exposition or commentary on a parable without any sense of its basic theme or message will not be helpful. A discussion of this sort without any reference to the plan, purpose, or central meaning of the parable would be ludicrous. Avoid a superficial approach in your interpretation. That's the reason careful research and exegesis are essential.

4. Seek to discover the central teaching of the parable. Investigate the parable to determine what is the most

urgent and essential kernel of truth. Don't waste all your time on minor details that keep you so busy or distracted that you never focus on the central thrust of the parable. Some preachers make the mistake of trying to find some significance in every detail in the parable. That may lead you on a side street and take you away from the main highway. You, of course, may have minor movements in the sermon, but hopefully they will lead to the central theme. The central theme of most of the parables focuses on the kingdom of God and the nature or characteristics of one who is a part of that kingdom.

5. Once you discover the central theme of the parable, don't turn the sermon into a trite moral on that truth. Jesus' parables are not simple stories conveying simple moral truths about life. In the parable of the talents, for example, don't reduce the parable to a moral like "faithfulness is all God demands of us." Moral and ethical teachings are clearly taught in many of the parables, but the preacher should avoid reducing any parable to a predetermined moralizing.

6. Remember that no one parable will contain the entire Christian message or a complete summary of Christian faith. A particular parable may teach only one facet or dimension of the Christian message. One may focus on love, another on judgment; another on hope; another on forgiveness; another on faithfulness, etc. The parable of the prodigal son may teach about forgiveness but not about faithfulness or judgment. Other teachings of Jesus will have to be considered to determine those themes.

7. Sometimes we may miss the teaching in a parable because we do not recognize that Jesus was using humor. Elton Trueblood found at least thirty parables of Jesus that he said used humor to communicate the message. Some of the parables of Jesus may have been poking fun

or making light of religious leaders or using humor to help the listener sense the meaning of the story without being totally offended.

8. In order to interpret a parable in our contemporary setting, one has to determine what the text meant originally in its day. The preacher should strive to understand the original meaning of the text — what did it mean in its day to the hearers of Jesus — before one can preach about what it means for our day.

9. Once the preacher has discovered the basic truth Jesus intended for a parable in his day, the preacher now has to determine how he or she will communicate that same truth in a way that will be clear, understandable, and applicable to the contemporary world today. The preacher has to discern what the text meant and what it continues to mean for us today.

10. Try to discover the surprising or unexpected lesson that Jesus was often trying to communicate in his parables. Many listeners would be startled to discover how refreshing the teachings of Jesus are when seen in this way. Jesus' imagery hangs in the listeners mind and startles him or her with its freshness or vitality. This approach tries to bring the listener to see through the window of the parable how the truth applies to him or her. Our preaching should try to preach the "teaching event," to enable the listener to experience in our day what the listener may have felt in his day. The words of preaching strive to cause a happening again.

The parables, to use Helmut Thielicke's phrase, are God's "picturebook."[4] These stories open the mind and heart and enable the listeners to grasp Jesus' message about the kingdom of God and its relationship to life. These ancient stories are still as modern as today's newspaper or the internet. The contemporary hearer can still see himself or herself in the "picturebook" when

---

4 Helmut Thielicke, *The Waiting Father*, (New York: Harper & Row, 1959), 11.

they are invited to enter the stories and discover the truth God has for them within. My prayer is that the modern preacher will proclaim them in a way that keeps that invitation open to the listeners.

Lessons From A Dishonest Man

(Parable of the Dishonest Manager)

Luke 16:1-13

What a rogue this man was that Jesus praised in this parable. It's really a rather unbelievable story, if you read it carefully. Jesus was praising a crook. I am sure, as the disciples heard that story, they were aghast. When he was first telling the story, they were probably waiting for the moral that he would drive home, like — "Now let me tell you how not to be like that guy." But Jesus surprised them by praising the man's shrewdness. There is no question that the man was a crook, so do not try to act like he was some nice guy. The man was indeed a crook, and I think Jesus knew exactly what he was trying to do with that story.

A Difficult Parable

We do not always know what to do with this parable. That has been the problem down through the centuries. In fact, some have found the story so difficult, confusing, and embarrassing that they have used it as evidence to demonstrate that the Christian faith really is unworthy of belief. The emperor Julian, who claimed to be a Christian and then fell away from the faith, used this very story as an example of the impossibility of trying to follow the teachings of Jesus.

Elton Trueblood has said that we do not understand the story because it is really humorous. The way Jesus told the story, according to Trueblood, indicates that the main point of the story is revealed in a sarcastic way.[5] Jesus really meant the opposite of what He said. It was tongue in cheek. We do this sometimes with each other. We tell some kind of story or tale and expect the response to be the very opposite of what we said. This parable

---

5 Elton Trueblood, *The Humor of Christ*, (New York: Harper & Row, 1964), 101f.

makes us squirm and twist to try to find the solution to the problem.

A Daring Story

As much as I admired Trueblood, I am not sure that he is on target here. I think Jesus was telling the story and meant it in a straightforward way. It was a daring imaginative attempt to use a very unlikely person as a hero. Jesus had done that on other occasions. The Good Samaritan, used as a hero, was an absolute surprise to the listener in the way Jesus used him in another story. They had not expected that this half-breed would be made a hero for them. On another occasion Jesus used an unrighteous judge as a leading character. This judge was continuously bombarded by a woman so many times that he thought she would black his eye. Finally, he responded and said: "Okay, I will do whatever you want." Jesus used a very unlikely hero in this parable to teach us lessons.

We have to remember that the parables are not allegories. Every person in a parable does not represent someone else. The master in this one is not a representative of God. The steward is not a representative of Jesus. In an allegory like *Pilgrim's Progress*, each character represents some religious or moral truth. This is not necessarily true in a parable. A parable seeks to make a particular emphasis or one point. Let us see if we can discover what that emphasis is in this parable.

A Glance At The Story

Look at the story. Here is a Jewish man who knows it is against the law of his own nation to collect interest. Since it is against his own laws and tradition, he will not do that. He is above that. So, what does he do? He hires a Gentile steward to do this task for him. Of course, he is not breaking the Jewish law, you understand, he is just using a heathen, a Gentile, to do that for him. He hired this man to oversee his business which was probably caring for some farms which he rented to other men. As the overseer, the steward simply rented the property to them.

As custom was in the eastern tradition, there was a certain rental fee, but everybody knew that one had to pay bribes underneath the table. I am told that this still goes on sometimes in that part of the world even today. Back in biblical times, it was a known policy that this is what one had to do to conduct business. The big boss, of course, would stand for that so long as it did not affect his business or hurt his reputation. If the manager got too greedy, and the renters felt they were being overcharged, or if he had to dip into the master's storehouse and take some of his grain to deal with these guys, then the boss realized he was losing not only goods but his reputation. If this happened, he knew he would have to dismiss the steward, because not only was he not a good manager but he was hurting his reputation. In the cases mentioned in our text, he obviously knew that is what happened. The owner came to the steward and said: "You are not doing a good job. I have to get somebody else."

What does this man do now that he will lose his job? He is shrewd. Jesus lets us inside the steward's mind and we overhear his conversation with himself. Listen to the steward as he says to himself: "Now, I cannot beg. I am too ashamed to do that. I cannot do manual labor. I am too old. I've got soft hands and I've gotten heavy around the waistline. I just cannot do physical work. So, what can I do?" He decided to call his renters in very suddenly, and you notice he did this before anybody got the word that he was no longer the manager. He asked one: "How much do you owe?" To the one who owed a thousand gallons of olive oil, he said: "Write it five hundred." No one can guess how much under the table he had been receiving, but evidently it was a large amount. He reduced that man's debt by fifty percent. He would probably still be making some money, even after that cut. He called the next renter in and he asked: "How much do you owe?" "A thousand bushels of wheat," he responded. "Cut it to eight hundred," the manager stated.

Notice that he seems to know the limits he could go with each of these men. Each one was not treated the same. He brought his owner an exact statement from the renters, which he probably had not had in writing before. In that day, a lot of deals were simply by word of mouth. Now he had in a written form what the renters' debts were. All of this was done to gain the favor of these renters whom he hoped would help him later. When his boss found out what he had done, he praised the steward for his ability to be resourceful. That is where the problem hits us clearly today. Jesus praised this guy for being a shrewd crook. What are we to make of this story? I would suggest several things.

Not A Lesson About How To Be Dishonest

For one thing, I do not think for a second that Jesus told this story to teach us to be dishonest. I believe he was trying to tell his disciples that we can learn some great truths on how to live in the world, even from people who are dishonest. The first lesson we can learn here is that a Christian is to be resourceful. Why is it that we will let crooks and dishonest people be more resourceful than the children of light? The Christians who are contrasted with the children of darkness are often much less resourceful than they are. Jesus is saying that we need to learn how to be more resourceful.

We admire resourceful crooks we see in movies or television shows. Do you remember several years ago a television show called *The Fugitive* which was later made into a movie? The series and movie focused on a man who spent part of life running from and evading the law. He was shrewd. Do you remember the movie about *The Dirty Dozen* who were taken from a prison and utilized by the US Military to carry out a dangerous mission? In *The Sting* with Paul Newman and Robert Redford, several crooks pull a twist on some other crooks in an intriguing story. Viewers were continuously amused on MASH when Hawkeye fooled the supply sergeant out of a box of medicine, a jeep or something else. America's "Most Wanted" or "Unsolved Mysteries" often reveals deceptive ways which we may not like, but we have to acknowledge the shrewdness which many often use to accomplish a dishonest goal. The news has often spoken about the resourcefulness of crooks.

Leslie Weatherhead, an English clergyman, was a soldier years ago in Arabia. He said that their battalion learned rather quickly how very resourceful some of the Arabs were. At nighttime, the British soldiers would sleep with their pistols under their bedroll and the next morning their pistols would be gone. Nobody's sleep was disturbed in the slightest. They began to wrap their rifle straps around their wrists and buried them partially under the ground beneath their bedroll when they went to sleep. The next day, many of the rifles would be gone. The soldiers would never be disturbed. Finally, two of the officers decided that they would sit up and watch for the Arabs as they tried to slip into their camp. The officers lay on the ground in the moonlight watching for the thieves who might sneak into camp. The two officers lay there all night long, and they never saw a soul come or go. The next morning, when they went back to their tent, all of the contents of their tent were gone. The captain of this particular group not only talked to these soldiers about what had happened, but he noted the resourcefulness of the enemy in this situation.

We have to admire these people, even if they were thieves, because they are so resourceful in the way they can get what they want. Jesus is not encouraging us to do what they are doing, but he is directing us to learn how to use our resourcefulness and intellect in all we seek to do in his cause. One of the keys for understanding this parable is the phrase, "For the children of this world are, in their generation, wiser than the children of light." An ancient proverb states that, "It is lawful to learn, even from an enemy."

I am amazed sometimes at how men and women can give hours and hours in learning how to play tennis or golf more effectively or how to fish better, or how to play football or basketball better. They will pour hours of time, effort, and energy to build these resources. That is commendable. Yet these same people will give almost no time or attention to the business of the church. Many will pour time, effort, and energy into almost everything else, and then we wonder why the Christian church has such a small impact in the world. We often do not use our resources to enable

Christianity to influence society. We need to let God work in and through us so we may be more useful for him with the resources which we have.

Learning To Look Ahead

Notice secondly that this man is praised because he looked ahead. In Moffat's translation of this passage, he speaks about Jesus' praising the man for his use of "unrighteous mammon." He does not translate the passage, "he used it wisely," but "he planned ahead." We need to look ahead and learn from the world how to be better and more effective Christians. To try to operate a church in an un-businesslike fashion or to carry out church work without order or discipline ends in chaos. Other places in society teach us to learn to use order and discipline as we plan ahead. We can draw on the best minds in the world to learn how to do things more effectively. We do not model the world's ethical standards and images, but we can learn from them efficiency in all we do.

I heard of a man in Washington, DC, who got into a taxicab and the cabby asked him, "Where do you want me to take you?" The man said, "Anywhere. It doesn't make any difference. I've got business everywhere." Now, to me, that is a part of our problem. Where do you want to go? For many, it is just any and everywhere and no place in particular. Our lives need direction and focus. Goals are essential to meaningful living. Sometimes the church itself has no sense of identification or direction. Often, as a church, we have no sense of who we are as a people. We also have no awareness of what we can become. We often have no real understanding of what Christ has enabled us to be. We seldom have a sense of our resources and gifts. In our struggle to understand the Christian life, clarity comes with a definite goal before us. Christ pulls us toward that goal to be his people on a mission in the world to do and to be what he has called us to be.

Business pours millions of dollars into research so it can plan ahead. They want to anticipate what customers' needs and wants are. Research, preparation, and imagination are used in almost every area of life, and these qualities need to be in the church in our preparation and employment of ministry. We should use the best minds that we can find to see how we can serve Christ today and in the future to be his church in the world, and in this particular place. Our church will always need a vision committee to dream, to set goals and directions for our church to minister effectively in our downtown location. We need to seek ways to minister efficiently in this century.

A Sunday school teacher was attempting to talk to his students one day and decided that he would ask them a question to begin the class. He turned to them and asked, "Why do you think people call me Christian?" One of the boys said, "Because they do not know you very well." Many of us sometimes find that people who know us well may not want to put that label on us. It ought to be the truth that the better you know someone, the more evident is his or her Christian characteristics. As Christians, we draw upon the power of Christ in our lives and it should be reflected in our business life, recreational life, and in all of our life. Hopefully others can see that we are authentically who we appear to be. As Christians, who live in today's world, we draw upon resources from wherever we find them and use them in the service of Christ. We do not bring the world's standards into the church and simply copy them. There is too much of that already in some churches. But we learn from the world and use the power of Christ to enable us to follow his wish, desire, and goal in using these contemporary resources.

Ernest Poole, in a novel titled *The Harbor*, tells about a young boy in Brooklyn Heights who used to walk down to look at the harbor, not too far from his home. He had to walk across a whole nest of train tracks and often the freight trains would be lined up so thick on the tracks and loaded down with their cargo that he could not even see the harbor. He said one night he learned that when he could not see the harbor for the freight trains that if he would just lift his eyes, he could see the stars above the trains. Some of us never get beyond the freight trains. We never see the harbor, and we never see the stars because we have never learned to lift our eyes. We focus too much just on the immediate problems. We focus primarily on the immediate needs. We focus only on what is right in front of us instead of seeing the goal which Christ is calling us to reach for as his church in the world. As we lift our eyes above the immediate needs, we experience the Christ who is calling us to greater avenues of ministry.

Getting Our Values Right

Third, I think Jesus is also telling us in this parable that we need to get our values right. Here is a man, when he got in a crunch in his life, saw that the most important thing to him was not money but friends. "Make friends by use of your material possessions." He attempted then, to use his ability with money to increase his friendships. Jesus teaches us through this parable to learn to use our financial resources so that we can develop friendships through them. This manager, of course, was concerned with a selfish end. I do not think Jesus is trying to tell us to use our financial resources selfishly. He used the phrase, "How much more." If this dishonest man used his opportunity selfishly, Jesus goes on to say, "how much more" we as Christians should learn to use our material resources for better ends. There is an old saying that states it this way: "What earthly good are you doing for heaven's sake?"

Some of us need to ask, "What good does our wealth and possessions do us? Are they directed toward any kind of end that is more than just something that is done selfishly for ourselves? Am I seeking to use whatever material possession I have so they can benefit and serve other people? The astonishing thing is that when we learn to use them in ways that reach out and touch the lives of others, we are not deliberately using our resources with selfish intents. But this approach builds for us genuine friendships. As we learn to use whatever resources we have to meet the needs of others around us, the astonishing thing is that we will draw them to us as friends. That is not our intent, but it is the result.

Money can be for us a master, an enemy, or a servant. Money can be for us a god, an idol. Money in and of itself is not evil. Paul writes about the love of money as the root of evil. When money becomes one's god, it becomes the chief end. Money can be used in service and ministry for God. Wouldn't it be astonishing if we could take a bill from our pocket, say a twenty-dollar bill, and it could talk to us and tell us about its journeys? That twenty-dollar bill might tell us that it was used at one time by an alcoholic and it brought him to his sad end. It might tell us that it was used at one time to purchase a lottery ticket. It might tell us that it was dropped in an offering plate to help build a church. It may have been given to a poor man who was hungry. It may have been given to a person who was thirsty, or it was given to meet a particular need. It might tell us it was used selfishly or illegally. Money can be used in all kinds of ways. Will money be our master, our god, our enemy, or will it be for us a servant which we can utilize to love and glorify God more effectively? Hopefully, it will be the latter.

You and I cannot build our lives on material possessions. Material possessions are not an end — they are a means. Let whatever our material possessions are become a resource, an avenue, a vehicle, a means of finding a better more meaningful life.

How Much More

This leads me to a fourth lesson in this parable. Jesus says that if this dishonest man has done this act for the wrong reason, "how much more" should we be able to learn the significance of little deeds in serving God? "If you are trustworthy in a little, you will be trustworthy in much." Think of the importance of a coin, a gift, a handshake, a smile, a thought, a concern, an embrace, a few moments of time, a telephone call, or a note. The little things we do indicate something about us in how we handle the big things of life. In businesses, most people fail sometimes not because they forget to handle the big decisions, but because they forget to do the daily things. They do not carry on the job effectively day after day. The big moments they may do well. But the little, everyday things many people often fumble along the way. Could that be one of the reasons for our economic crisis today? Was a part of the problem that banks overlooked the "small" fact that those who wanted loans did not have enough income to finance the loan, and there was no insurance behind the loans if the borrower couldn't repay the loan? Small matters can be very significant! We need to learn to use the small opportunities to hear how God is expecting us to draw upon them to grow in our lives.

When we read the scriptures, we find that God often enabled people, through their use of some small or seemingly insignificant things, to make some gigantic advances for him. Moses stood before Pharaoh with nothing but a staff in his hand. With a shepherd's staff in hand, he declared to Pharaoh, "God says let my people go." That staff symbolized to Moses that the power of God was present with him. David crossed a brook and picked up a few stones and then stood before a great giant who was threatening the army of Israel, and he said to the Philistine giant that he had come to confront him in the name of God. He had only a sling and a few stones, yet the power of God was conveyed through a stone. Jesus took a few fish and a few pieces of bread, blessed and broke them, feeding a multitude.

Years later, Florence Nightingale had just a few pills and bandages, but she started the nursing movement that soon reached around the world. Albert Schweitzer went to a far remote corner of the world. Many people thought that this great scholar had dropped off the edge of the earth. But his deeds, which were done in this small obscure place, were soon echoed around the world.

All of these small symbols or services had an effect that reached out to the world far beyond the smallness of their beginning. What you do in your Sunday school class; what you do through youth work; what you do as you care for your children week by week; a visit to a homebound or a sick person in a nursing home; what you do as you sing in the choir; what service you render as an usher; what you do as you count the money; what you do in hundreds of ways in this church and community may seem to some people to be small things, but they are giant things in the sight of God. The little services you render are indications of what you are really like inside.

There was a young boy who had been burned very badly in an accident. His family and friends were concerned about him. His teacher asked a tutor if she would go by and work with him. His teacher said, "In our class, we are studying irregular verbs and dangling participles. He will get so far behind that he will never catch up if someone doesn't help him." When the tutor went to the hospital, she did not realize that this young boy was still in the critical care unit because he had been so severely burned. He could barely talk. It was very difficult for her as she tried to teach this young lad that day about irregular verbs and dangling participles.

She left wondering what good she had done at all. The next day when she came back to the hospital, the head nurse met her with the biggest smile you have ever seen. "You will never know how much good you did yesterday," she said. "Why, what do you mean?" The nurse said, "I don't know what you said or did, but a big change has come over this boy. He seemed to have given up. But because of your being here, it has revolutionized him. He is working with us and seeking to get better."

Later after the young lad got well and went home, his family asked him what had happened that day. "You know, I was burned so badly that I did not think I had any hope at all of getting well," he responded. "I wondered what the point was in trying. Everybody told me that I was going to get well, but I really did not believe it. When this teacher came by and started teaching me about irregular verbs and dangling participles, I thought to myself later that night that nobody was going to waste their time teaching that stuff to somebody they think is dying. So, it gave me a sense of hope and faith." This teacher's effort seemed a small act, but it made all of the difference in that young boy's life.

Jesus is telling us that the smallest things that we do in our lives sometimes can make an unbelievable impact for good or evil. Jesus reminds us that we can learn even from dishonest people to be more resourceful, we can learn to look ahead, and to discover the value of using money correctly for higher ends than merely physical ones. How much more should we learn to be more resourceful than the children of darkness, since we belong to the children of light?

Today ask yourself: "Have I used my resources for God? Have I dedicated my gifts to his service? Am I using my money in ways to serve God and influence others to know his friendship?" Today, examine your own life and see where you are in your commitment to God. If you have not surrendered to him, let this be the moment you open your life to him and experience that redeeming grace. If you committed your life to him sometime in the past, renew that vow today. If you feel that you are burdened down, lean upon the power of God, and sense his sustaining grace. In the quietness of your seat or in a public way, take your stand for Christ.

Big Shots In The Church:

(Parable of the Cheap Seats)

Luke 14:7-11

The place — Uptown, USA. The occasion — The Man of the Year Awards Banquet. The time — the present. Everybody who was anybody was present for this big night. The people sitting on the lower level were busy trying to see who was seated at the head table. There at the head table sat Loretta Lovely, Perry Prosperous, Tom Talkative, a local TV announcer, and the Reverend Peter Pious, pastor of Peach Protestant Church. Harry Hilarity, was the emcee for the night. Hugh Haughty was seated next to Sam Self-Righteous and Henrietta Highhat. Next there was Mayor Marvin Moneybags. Governor Kevin "Keep the People" Confused was on the mayor's right. Judge Jake Justice of the Rich and Famous sat next to him. They were followed by Richard Rich, Fred Famous, Rhonda Realtor, Sophia Superficial, Peter Practical, Desmond Deception, Dr. Marvin Medicine, and Mr. Macho Muscles — the famous football player. Filling out the table was General George Gallantry, Preston Patriotic, and Conrad "Climb the Corporate" Ladder. All of the people of community worth were there.

The host for this special occasion, Walter Wealthy, looked over the distinguished guests sitting at the head table. He noticed that something wasn't right. He looked around and finally asked: "Where is Larry Lowly? Where is Larry Lowly?" From way back in the cheap seats, a hand went up. I'm sitting back here." "Larry, you are the main guest," Mr. Wealthy said. "What are you doing way back there? Come up here to the head table." Then Mr. Wealthy looks down at the head table and all the dignitaries sitting there. Then he notices that Ronnie Run Over Everybody to Reach the Top is sitting in one of the chief seats at the banquet table. "Ronnie," the host exclaims, you will have to go down there where Larry was sitting. Larry, you come up here and sit at the main table where Ronnie was."

This tongue-in-cheek story is a humorous attempt to use a method similar to what Jesus employed in his presentation of this parable about people seeking chief seats at a marriage feast. By the method of this parable, Jesus used humor and whimsical means as he often did to disarm people so he might present a truth to them about God and life.

The Banquet Layout

Banquets in Jesus' day were considered very special occasions, especially a marriage feast. Several tables were normally put together in a U-shape for a banquet of this type. The host would be seated in the center of the table. The most distinguished guest would be at his immediate right. The next distinguished guest would be to his left. The next most distinguished guest would usually be next and so on around the table. If someone had taken a distinguished guest's place, he likely had to be asked to move to a place at the table further away from the host. You also need to be aware that people didn't sit in chairs around the table like we do today. They reclined on their elbow on top of benches around the table.

Jesus used this occasion not to give a lesson in social etiquette, but to teach a parable about the kingdom of God — our relationship to God and other people. Unfortunately, we think we can rush in and seize the chief seats in God's kingdom. Jesus instructs us in this parable that the chief seats in God's kingdom cannot be seized. They are gifts from God, acquired through humble service.

The Problem of Pride

This parable, like other passages in the scriptures, teaches us about the constant battle between humility and pride in our lives. As we look around, we are keenly aware that pride is not a problem confined to the ancient world. From almost the time we were born, we have been filled with a sense of pride and self-importance. We are told to achieve — to strive to be number one.

Many begin teaching their children at a very young age that they ought to try to be at the top of their class. "Achieve first place," we urge. "Try to be the little league champs." "Be the head cheerleader or May Queen." "Be all-state and all-American." "Be Miss America or Mr. America." "Climb up the ladder." "Reach for the top." "Be in Who's Who." Usually colleges and seminaries line up the professors in graduation processions by their rank and seniority. Most businesses and organizations have their chief seats with their throne rooms and board rooms where the important people gather to make decisions. The scriptures clearly tell us that pride is our paramount sin. Pride is idolatry. Self has usurped the place of God. I am the most important person in the world. Pride leads to idolatry when we begin to see all of life through our own glasses. We do not even see or recognize the concerns and needs of others. We see life primarily from the perspective of self-interest. Pride asserts itself as our God-almightiness where we parade around in our own peacock feathers to call attention to ourselves. We see this all the time as men and women grasp for the prize to be number one in whatever organization they are involved.

Pride gives birth to the sins of vanity, conceit, scorn, arrogance, and prejudice. Edwin McNeill Poteat, writing about this parable, observed: "To put it another way, God exalts man, man humbles himself. The importance of this is seen at once when it is reversed and the agencies are exchanged. Then man exalts himself and humbles God. This is not merely misbehaving at a banquet; it is committing the unpardonable sin of setting one's self in the place of God."[6] This is our God-almightiness — the attempt to put ourselves in God's rightful place. Our will seeks to bend his to shape our own desires. C. S. Lewis warns us when he writes: "If anyone would like to acquire humility, I can, I think, tell him the first step. The first step is to realize that one is proud. And a biggest step, too. At least, nothing whatever can be done before it. If you think you are conceited, it means you are very conceited

---

6 Edwin McNeill Poteat, *Parables of Crisis* (New York: Harper & Brothers, 1950), 91.

indeed."⁷ We have to begin with the acknowledgment of our basic sin of pride.

One of my favorite cartoonists is Doug Marlette. He used to draw a cartoon of a preacher, the Reverend Will B. Dunn. In one of the cartoons Will is seen dressed in his typical black suit and black hat. He is on his knees praying, and is obviously upset. "Lord?..." he prays. "Smite mine enemies, Lord... Smite 'em! Smite mine own worst enemy!" Then there is a large "Zap" as a lightning bolt comes down and hits him. In the last frame, he is burned and singed. He prays: "Let me rephrase that...."⁸ Through this cartoon, Doug Marlette is telling us that often we, WE are our own worst enemy. Pride — our own self-righteousness — destroys us.

The Power Of Humility

Humility is a great biblical virtue. The word humble comes from a root word which means ground or earth. The really humble person is aware that he/she is a creature. God has created us. God is the Creator. We belong to God. We are humble because we have an awareness of our place in the created order. This awareness doesn't mean that you see yourself as having no worth, or value, or that you are unimportant. Of course, you have value and significance. You are a child of God, who has been created by God. Jesus has reminded us that we should love our neighbor as ourselves. There is a healthy self-love. But self-love becomes sinful when the self gets so out of focus that we see life only from our limited perspective and are not able to see the needs of others at all. We have all seen self-love become twisted and distorted when individuals remain blinded by their narrow, selfish vantage point.

We also know that humility is not something one acquires like a trophy. There was a group that was having a contest one night to see who was the humblest. Finally, they decided to give the award of a humble pie to Betty Betters. When Betty went up

---

7 C.S. Lewis, *Mere Christianity* (New York: The Macmillan Co., 1965), 99.
8 Doug Marlette, There's No Business Like Soul Business (Atlanta: Peachtree Publishers, 1987).

to receive the pie as her reward for her humility, she lost it. Her willingness to accept the pie, they said, indicated that she was not really humble. Humility is such an elusive word, isn't it? Just when we think we are humble, we realize that we are not. Humility always slips out of our grasp. Jesus told a parable one day about a Pharisee who thought he was righteous. He likewise described a publican who felt that he was far from God. The irony was that the one who felt he was close to God was far away from him, while the one who felt he was far away from God was close to him. Humility is not something that one can grasp to his or her breast. If one thinks that he or she is humble, then that is clear evidence that one is not.

Linus and Charlie Brown are leaning against a wall talking. Linus says, "I'd like to make a lot of money, but I would hate to be a snob. I've given this a lot of thought." "So, what have you decided?" Charlie Brown asks. Linus replies, "So I have decided to be a very rich and famous person who doesn't really care about money, and who is very humble but who still makes a lot of money and is very famous, but is very humble and rich and famous." Charlie Brown says, "Good luck!"[9]

That is what we want, isn't it? But we have discovered long ago that humility is not so easily obtained. Humility is a trait that is developed in one's life as you and I acknowledge our openness to God's leadership. Jesus stated in his first beatitude, "Blessed are the poor in spirit, for theirs is the kingdom of God." Those who are poor before God open themselves to God to be filled by God's presence. J. B. Phillips has translated this beatitude in these words: "Happy are the humble-minded, for the kingdom of heaven is theirs!" Those who are truly humble are the ones who acknowledge their indebtedness to God and their need of God. We should not be like the Sunday school teacher who taught the parable on the Pharisee and publican to her young children and said: "Oh, let us now thank God that we are not like that nasty old Pharisee." The problem is we are too often like the Pharisee.

---

[9] Robert L. Short, *The Gospel According to Peanuts* (Richmond, Virginia: John Knox Press, 1965), 61.

The World's Standard For Greatness Material Wealth

What is the world's standard for judging greatness? The world often measures greatness by material wealth. What we have determines our greatness. We, like the rich farmer in another of Jesus' parables, build larger and bigger barns. Greatness from this vantage point is judged by how much you have in the bank, your number of stocks, and how many cars and houses you own. Material wealth is often the criteria used to judge whether a person is really great.

Strength Or Power

Secondly, society often judges a person to be famous or significant in terms of their strength or power. Sometimes this power or strength is evidenced in their ability to control industry, corporations, finance, or the stock market. Sometimes it is represented in a person's athletic ability or the military power of a nation. Athletes become our heroes, and a "Rambo" type becomes our fantasy model for solving complex problems. The great are measured in their ability to exercise military power over other nations or dominate another person or company by force. These are seen as the great people. They are the movers and shakers in society. They are both admired and feared.

Intellectual Gifts

At other times, we judge a person as great by his or her intellectual gifts. Their wide or very focused knowledge and intellectual prowess set them apart in society. They are the masters in our research centers and at our computer keyboards. But we sometimes forget that Germany and Japan were both great intellectual nations; look at the havoc that they reaped on the world. Intellect alone is not sufficient.

God's Standard Of Greatness

God uses a different standard for judging greatness. God measures greatness by a person's humility. You can't measure whether a person is genuinely great merely by using the standards of wealth, power, prestige, and intellectual gifts. The Bible offers us a different standard altogether. A truly great person is aware of his or her need and dependence upon God. This awareness results in a genuine sense of humility. Humility becomes a doorway to meet God. Pride closes the door, while humility opens the door. The first requirement of authentic religion is for a person to acknowledge his or her need of God. This can't be done without humility. The truly great person is humble.

Limited Knowledge

A humble person is also aware of what limited knowledge he or she has. We should know that we have only scratched the surface of knowledge. How dare any person flaunt arrogantly that he or she is really a wise person! The most brilliant people have dipped only a small bucket in the ocean of knowledge. What we have in our "buckets" is minuscule compared to the oceans of ignorance that we still have about the world around us and within us. We look through a microscope and we see that there is still a whole world waiting to be more fully explored. We look through our telescopes and we are still discovering new planets and solar systems. The universe seems to be endless and expanding.

Who has all knowledge? Who is a thoroughly educated person? Here is a man who writes brilliant books, but he couldn't grow a thing in the ground if his life depended on it. Here is a person who is great with his hands. He can fix anything mechanical, it doesn't make any difference what it is. But he can't even read. Here is a woman who can speak ten languages. She is brilliant in languages. But she couldn't cook a meal in the kitchen at all. Here is Joe Smith who is a master carpenter, but he can't begin to communicate with somebody else who talks a foreign tongue. Here is another person who is great in athletics, but he can't drive a nail. Do you hear it? A person can be intelligent, brilliant, able in one realm, but so ignorant in another. No matter how brilliant a person may be — he or she may understand the most complicated theories of physics, understand computers, and the vast intricacies of details which they can accomplish, and yet be abysmally ignorant in so many other realms of life.

When I was a professor at Southern Seminary in Louisville, Kentucky, it was always astonishing to me to see seminary students arrive on campus who already understood God, the scriptures, and theological systems completely. As freshmen, they came, they thought, equipped to teach their professors what they were to understand and believe. They presumed to sit in judgment on others as though they had the inside track on how to understand the nature and mind of God. As I get older and study more, the one thing that is so clear to me is my abysmal ignorance in every realm. I have only scratched the surface of knowledge. We always stand on the edge of mystery in every realm of life. This dictates that we should always be humble people. Arrogance should never be a part of our posture.

Human Frailty

Our own human frailty should remind us of our need for humility. We are so vulnerable. A slip in the bathtub, a drunken driver across the road and our life can be snatched away. A tiny virus can bring down the strongest athlete. A poorly constructed car, a defective part, an accident, a mistake in judgment can change our lives forever. Too much oxygen, not enough oxygen, too much water, not enough water can end our life. Our pain, sickness, aging, and grief should all make us aware of our own human frailty. Who can dare be arrogant when we never know at any moment when our own lives may slip away?

Our Indebtedness To Others

Humility reminds us of our indebtedness to so many other people. How can we ever be arrogant and claim that we are self-made people when we are all indebted to countless numbers of people? We are indebted to our parents for giving us birth and life, for the first years of our learning and for food, shelter, and love. We are indebted to our schoolteachers, professors, Sunday school teachers, friends, and strangers. We are indebted to carpenters, bricklayers, electricians, farmers, plumbers, grocery store owners, doctors, dentists, lawyers, and bankers. We are indebted to people for air conditioning and heat, for books, newspapers, televisions, computers, smart-phones, the internet, cars, planes, and houses. We are indebted to people in all walks of life, many of whom we do not even know. We take so many of these gifts for granted. But we should declare with Paul, "I am debtor both to the barbarian and to the Greeks, both to the wise and to the foolish" (Romans 1:14). Most of all, we are indebted to God for his gift of redemption. Salvation is God's gift, and we are indebted to him for such love.

Several years ago, I had the opportunity of visiting a church member who was no longer able to come to church. She taught children for more than fifty years in the preschool Sunday school department. Think! Think of all the children and parents who are indebted to this woman for her devotion and love through fifty years of ministry. The lives of countless children are forever different because of her contact with them. How can they ever pay her back? She and countless other quiet people serve God faithfully where they are. They do so without seeking recognition or reward.

The truly humble people acknowledge their indebtedness to others and God and in humble gratitude declare with George Matheson the hymn writer:

"I give thee back the life I owe
That in thine ocean depths its flow
May richer, fuller be."

Aware Of Our Own Needs

The truly humble people are aware of their own needs and confess their need before God and their dependence upon God. We acknowledge that God measures greatness with a different standard than the world uses. God's standard for greatness is measured by a person's humility. Too often we confuse being famous with being great. The world may use a different standard to depict greatness and ignore people who teach quietly in a Sunday school class, or teach in public school, offer medical service in rural America, or serve in some obscure place in our society. We may never hear of them. They may share their gifts with those whose lives they have touched and will never be the same again because of that contact, and "blush unseen" before the rest of the world.

Jonathan Edwards

One of the most prominent theologians in early American history was Jonathan Edwards. Edwards was born in 1703 and attended Yale when he was thirteen and graduated when he was only seventeen. After he finished seminary, he returned and tutored for a while at Yale. His grandfather was the pastor of a congregational church in Northampton, Massachusetts, and Edwards was called to serve as an assistant to his grandfather. Later when his grandfather died, Jonathan Edwards was called to be pastor of that church when he was only 26 years old. Things went well in the church for many years. This was the time of the great revival which swept across America. The church boomed for years. But in 1744 things began to take a different turn in the church. The revivalism enthusiasm faded. Nobody joined his church for four years. In 1750, the church asked for the pastor's resignation. At that time Jonathan Edwards was 47 years old, married, and the father of ten children! After he stepped aside, the church found that it wasn't easy to get another pastor. So, they asked him if he would come back and supply for them until they could get a new pastor. He did. Edwards graciously supplied for them until they secured a pastor.

Then the only congregation that would call Edwards was a small church in Stockbridge, Massachusetts. He went there and struggled to support his family and ministered to the Native Americans. While pastor of that obscure church, he wrote *Freedom of the Will* and some of his other great theological works. In 1757, he was called to be the president of New Jersey College, which later became Princeton. Jonathan Edwards was a humble man, who was willing to serve wherever God called him. He served in good times and in adverse circumstances, even when he was rejected. But he continued to serve God without complaint, and today history judges him as one of our great American theologians.

The Significance Of Service

When you and I seek to understand greatness in God's sight, we need to understand that greatness is judged by God in terms of service. What form does this ministry for Christ take? The church has a ministry that takes the form of a servant. Just as Jesus was obedient unto death, even the death on the cross, so he has called his disciples to a servant ministry. Jesus identified himself with the image of the suffering servant from Isaiah. He said, "I came not to be ministered unto, but to minister and to give my life a ransom for many." "If anyone would be first, he/she must be last of all." "The greatest of all is the servant of all" (Mark 10:44). Jesus took a towel and a basin and girded himself and washed the feet of his disciples. He indicated to them by this act what kind of ministry they should take — a servant ministry. Jesus said, "I have given you an example that you should do unto others as I have done unto you." His ministry was to be a servant. The church's ministry is to take the form of a servant in the world. The church is not to be served or to serve us, but to minister in the world in Christ's name. He has called us to a ministry not to see what we can get out of it for ourselves but what we can do in service for him. A servant of Christ will not be power hungry or status conscious; will not be divisive and seek merely to get his or her own way without concern for the church community. As a servant, he or she decreases that the master might increase.

Have you ever thought about some ministers or lay people who have served Christ in obscure, isolated places? These people have labored sometimes for years without a single convert. I heard about some missionaries who served for fourteen years in the Yukon before they ever had one single convert to Christ. Were they successful? It depends on how you measure success, doesn't it? God has not called us to be successful, but to be faithful in our ministry for him. We look back in history and we point to people like Francis of Assisi, Florence Nightingale, Albert Schweitzer, Lottie Moon, Ghandi, Martin Luther King, Jr., and Mother Teresa. These are people who gave their lives in service to a cause greater than themselves. They have attempted to minister in God's name, not to secure some place in history for themselves. "The greatest of all is the servant of all," our Lord reminds us.

The Burma Diary

Out of the Second World War there came a book called *The Burma Diary*. It was written in 1942 by a professor who had been a teacher at the University of Rangoon. During the war, the patients in one of the hospitals had to be moved to avoid the advancing Japanese army. Paul Geren, the professor, like many others, was assisting in this task. When he walked into the hospital to help, he discovered the filth and a stench from those who were suffering from dysentery. The endless rains and the inability to get clothing and bed linens dry made the assignments even more difficult. "A reeking stench like a burnt offering to some perverse deity," the author observed, "rose from the patients, the soiled bedding, and soiled clothing."

He, along with an American who had joined the British army before the United States got into the war, and a British soldier, stood looking at the ordeal which awaited them. "I am very glad at this moment," the American said to the British soldier, "that I am an agnostic."

"Since he did not believe in the love of Christ, he could leave the handling of these dysentery victims to the sweepers," Professor Geren observed. "Since his friend did believe in it, he was not free to stand by and watch. Nor was I," he affirmed. "Get down in it! Pick the patients up! .... There is no need to call this filthiness sweet, or to start enjoying it through a strange inversion. Only one thing is necessary: for love's sake, it must be done."[10]

God challenges us sometimes to go into dirty, difficult places to meet human need. It is not always easy, clean, or sweet. God judges greatness not by the world's standards. I think you and I may be absolutely amazed at those who will have crowns in heaven that will be filled with jewels beyond our understanding. These individuals served God in quiet places, giving of themselves faithfully, serving humbly, and maybe without any

---

10 Paul Geren, *Burma Diary* (New York: Harper & Brothers, 1943), 51-52.

recognition at all. "The greatest of all is the servant of all," our Lord instructed. "Do not seek the chief seats," Jesus said. He has called us to minister. Let's be about the work that God has called us to do.

When Going To Church Dosen't Mean Much

(Parable of the Pharisee and the Publican)

Luke 18: 9–14

The listeners sat in stunned silence as Jesus finished the parable. They did not understand it. It was a complete reversal of everything they had believed. The Pharisee, the righteous one, was condemned by another religious leader. The publican, the one they saw as chief among sinners, was praised. They simply did not understand that story at all. They sat in shocked disbelief.

Look Again At This Old Story
Two men went up to the temple to pray. Just as they did in the day of Jesus, so today, two men go up to the temple to pray. Two women go to church to pray. You and somebody else go to church to pray. Be careful how quickly you judge the motives of the Pharisee. Be careful how quickly you condemn him and say, "Oh, isn't he bad?" You have gone up to church this day. Two men, two women, young people have all gone up to church today. Why? Some of you have come to see your friends. Some of you are in church just because it is a habit. Some of you come to hear the music. Some of you go to hear the sermon. Some of you go to church because you think it is a good thing to do. Some come only out of curiosity or others out of a deep need. I wonder how many men, women, or young people have gone up to church to pray — to worship. The word pray here in the New Testament, can also mean worship.

What Was A Pharisee?
The Pharisee has gotten a lot of bad press, hasn't he? The New Testament is not very nice to the Pharisee. He is condemned repeatedly. But the Pharisees were some of the finest, most respected men in their community. They were deeply devout

and pious people. They prayed at set times, several times a day. They fasted not just occasionally, but twice a week. Rather than a heavy man as he has often been depicted, the Pharisee would be lean and trim from his times of fasting. He was a man of self-discipline. His life was well-controlled. He believed in the Bible and took every word in it literally. He was a fine moral person. He was somebody that you would want to do business with, because his word could be trusted. When you shook hands with him, you knew that his handshake meant something.

This was a truly moral person, and you could take him at his word. He was a man who was devoted to his family. There was never any scandal that surrounded his life. He was indeed a man of high moral principles. He also was a man who was generous with his money. He not only gave to the temple what the law required, but he went far beyond that. There were some items which Moses had restricted from the tithe. But he tithed everything. There was none of his income or possessions on which he did not tithe. He gave more than was required. He was a very generous man, highly moral, and well respected in the community.

The Separated One

But he was also a tragic figure, especially as he is depicted in this parable by Jesus. Look at the prayer of the Pharisee. He probably went up to the temple on a special holy day, maybe the Day of Atonement. As he goes up to pray, he looks around and notices the other people gathered there for worship. He sees the publican and he puts as much distance between himself and others as he possibly can. The word Pharisee means "the separated one." He avoided contact with others because he feared that he might accidentally brush against someone like the publican and be unclean and have to devote weeks of special prayer and fasting to cleanse himself from this uncleanliness. He keeps his distance from others. So too, do some today. They will not rub elbows with some people even in church. They keep a little distance between themselves and others. They do not speak to them nor are they really concerned about them. They stand apart.

A Holy Telegram

The Pharisee prays aloud. As someone has said, he sends a "holy telegram" to God. He preaches instead of praying. He begins his prayer, as he has been taught, with thanksgiving. But what is his prayer of thanksgiving? "I thank you God," he says, "that I am not like other men." His prayer reveals one who is very conceited. Here is a man who is enamored with himself. The focus is primarily about what he has done. "I... I... I "echoes again and again through his prayer. Rather than his words flowing smoothly, they are almost like a flat tire which causes a car to go bumping along as his "I's" are lifted up toward God. Rabbi Simeon once said, "If there are only two holy men, my son and I are those two. If there is only one, I am he." This Pharisee obviously felt that way. It was Spurgeon who said that there was a man in his congregation whom he thought to be the most holy man he ever knew until the man told him about his holiness.

In his prayer, the Pharisee lifts up himself, talks about himself and what he has done to pile up good works before God. His conceit is overwhelming. We are told that we can tell what people are like by the books they read, by the movies they see and by the company they keep. I think it would also be true to say that you can know men, women, and young people by their prayers. If we could hear how other people pray in private, it might be a tremendous revelation of what they are really like. Here this Pharisee exposes himself fully. Instead of looking through a window that opens into God, he looks into a mirror and sees only a reflection of himself.

Tries To Put God In His Debt

The Pharisee is a tragic figure, because he thought he could make God indebted to him by what he had done. He assumed he could put God in his debt, so God would have to do something for him in return. "I have tithed," he said. I have done certain things; therefore, God is in my debt." But is the Pharisee a stranger to us?

I hear conversations like that almost daily: "Why did this happen to me? I do not understand it. I attend church regularly. I pray. I read my Bible. I give to the church. Why did my husband get sick?" Do you hear what is being said? I have done this, God is supposed to do that.

We hear it on other levels as well. "I don't understand it," a wife says. "I prepare my husband's meals, I wash and iron his clothes. I keep the house clean, but he really doesn't care for me." The husband says, "I provide the paycheck. I work my fingers to the bone, but my wife doesn't care for me." They both assume that because they have done something for the other, that person is now obligated to them. Where is love in all of this? Where is a relationship of caring and concern? Their relationship unfortunately is built only on obligation and indebtedness. We can't pile up merit before God if we come to church seven days a week. If we give nine-tenths of everything we have, we can't make God obligated to us. That is not to say you shouldn't worship. That is not to say you shouldn't come to church, but you don't do it just to make God indebted to you. We worship out of thanksgiving, a sense, a need and a desire to praise God.

The Sin Of Self-Righteousness

The Pharisee was guilty of sin. His sin was self-righteousness. His sin was pride, which is the most basic sin. This "holy" man stood in church to pray. Nevertheless, he was a sinner. His basic sin was pride, his god-almightiness. "I am better — I am holier than others," he reasoned to himself. This man, even in church, was very irreligious, and he never knew it. He thought he was close to God, yet he was very far from God.

In the "Peanuts" comic strip, Linus was listening to the radio. Lucy comes walking in and says, "I don't want to listen to that station. I want to listen to my station." "I think I'll go upstairs and listen to a record," Linus responds. While he is listening to his record, Lucy walks up and says, "I don't want to listen to that record. I want to listen to my record." "I think I'll watch television," Linus says. So, he goes in and turns on the television set. Lucy walks in and declares, "I don't want to watch that program. I want to watch my program." Finally, Linus says, "I believe I will go outside and look at the stars." She follows him outside and says, "I don't want to look at your stars, I want to look at my..." Then she stops. "They are never 'my' stars, are they?"

Many of us go through life that way. We surround ourselves with a sense of "my-ness." This is the "me" generation. All of life revolves around "me," my needs, my wishes, my desires, my goals, my aims, my satisfaction, my drives, and my intents. The basic sin of pride is still evident in church. And it is clearly seen when a person asserts his or her self-righteousness. They are proud of their own goodness. They have self on the throne and not God.

When Comparisons Fail

The Pharisee compares himself with others and he points to the Publican — the tax collector — in particular and declares: "I am not like other men who are extortionists, robbers, and adulterers. I am better than they are. I am certainly not like this publican." Comparisons can always be easy, can they not? I know that I can find somebody whom I think I am better than, and so can you. But there will always be somebody else somewhere who will be better than you or I. You may not always be the best doctor, best attorney, best teacher, the best mother, the best husband, the best father, the best wife, or the best whatever. When we compare ourselves to somebody else, any of us can make ourselves look superior to another. It is easy to find someone we stand above, isn't it? That is especially true, when, like the Pharisee, we select somebody whom we think is not very moral. Compared to them, we feel we measure up rather highly. When we set our own standards, we can always reach them. When we aim at the gutter or slightly above it for our moral standards, we can always make it. But when we begin to reach for the highest standard — to be like God — that becomes an impossible goal that challenges us to reach for the highest possible goal in life.

What is the standard for whiteness? How white is white? I used to drive by a white frame house that appeared to be beautifully white. But I remember one winter when a snow fell and covered the ground around that house. After the snow had first fallen, it was amazing how the whiteness of the house looked gray compared to the whiteness of the snow. I can appear very righteous compared to somebody else. If I set my own standard, what a good boy I can declare myself to be! Look at the Pharisee again. He was not guilty of any gross sin, but he was guilty of the most basic sin which is pride. He says, "I am not like that publican." But he was also not much like God. He was not like the publican, but he wasn't like God either. God does not want us to see ourselves in a selfrighteous, superior, holier than thou manner either. Instead of seeing ourselves as better than others, we are challenged to reach out to people in need and minister to them.

Being Irreligious In Church

Unlike the Sunday school teacher I mentioned earlier, who taught the parable about the publican and Pharisee to a Sunday school class and said that "we are not supposed to be like the nasty old Pharisee, the lesson, in reality, is that we are too often the Pharisee. You and I are the Pharisees. Jesus would be telling us today that we can be irreligious in church and we can be serving God for the wrong reasons. Our motives will not always be correct. Unfortunately, this has been true down through the history of Israel and through much of the ministry of the church.

There are times that going to church doesn't mean much. Jeremiah the prophet stood before the congregation of Israel and told them:

You keep saying, "This place is the temple of the Lord, the temple of the Lord, the temple of the Lord." This catchword of yours is a lie; put no trust in it. Mend your ways and your doings, deal fairly with one another, do not oppress the alien, the orphan, and the widow, shed no innocent blood in this place, do not run after other gods to your own ruin. Then will I let you live in this place, in the land which I gave long ago to your forefathers for all time. You gain nothing by putting your trust in this lie. You steal, you murder, you commit adultery and perjury, you burn sacrifices to Baal, you run after other gods whom you have not known; then you come and stand before me in this house, which bears my name, and say, "We are safe," — safe, you think, to indulge in all these abominations. Do you think that this house, this house which bears my name, is a robber's cave? (Jeremiah 7:4-11 The New English Bible).

He warned them that they could not live immoral lives and expect to walk back into the temple and be magically cleansed. He told them that they did not understand what the temple of God was.

When Religion Falls Short

There are times when going to church doesn't mean much. Not everything that is done in the name of religion is good. The Reformation was a protest against the indulgences which the church sold to cleanse people from their sins. Sometimes, the method which the Pope employed to raise money for his building programs was wrong. There are people today who are raising money in the name of God in a way that is wrong. Any and everything cannot be justified in the name of religion.

Several years ago, in another church, I had a man call me up one day and advise me that he wanted to give some money to the church and designate it to be used to pay for his father's expenses in a nursing home and count it as a designation to the church. I said, "I'm sorry, but you can't do that." "What do you mean?" he asked. "Why can't I do it?" "It is not legal," I said. "You can't do it." I knew from personal experience that this was not permitted because my wife's father was in a nursing home at that very time.

There are some people who want to give to the church for the wrong reasons — to get a deduction on their income tax. They are not concerned about the church, God, or religion. It is certainly all right to take your contribution to your church as a deduction on your income tax. But that should not be your reason for giving. Sometimes we can give for the wrong reasons. Our motives sometimes become confused.

Sometimes Church Doesn't Mean Much

We have to be honest and acknowledge that there are times when going to church doesn't mean much. Some go to church and won't speak to another. They gossip and spread lies behind their back. They sit through church and then go out into the world and live an immoral and dishonest life. Being in church will not automatically make us clean. We may leave with dirty minds and hearts. Mark Barton, who several years ago killed his wife, children and nine other people, attended church. Going to church will not automatically cure mental and emotional problems, nor keep someone from harming others if they do not live by the moral principles they are taught. We need to repent of our sins, change our ways and experience forgiveness. Sometimes we need to seek professional help. We may come to church and leave with self still on the throne instead of God. We need to open ourselves to God and be cleansed by God's forgiving grace. If not, going to church doesn't mean much.

There was a young minister who finally resigned his church and walked away from it one day. The telling blow that convinced him that he could no longer serve that church came in a business session when one of the members stood up and said: "I am tired of the minister telling us that we ought to do the Christian thing; what we need to do is what is best for our church." There are churches which often take un-Christian action in the name of religion. Remember, going to church may not mean very much.

Using Prayer For A Selfish Goal

I enjoy ballgames as much as anyone. Maybe I am one of the oddballs in life, but I am not thrilled at all when an athlete says, "Everything I have accomplished is because of prayer in my life. My ability on the athletic field has come about through prayer." I am not impressed with that because it is a way of declaring that God is obligated to me because of my prayer life. Prayer becomes a magical means of achieving a selfish end. I know that I can never become a better athlete through prayer.

Prayer is no shortcut to stardom. A person is a good athlete because of his or her training, skills, discipline, coaching, gifts, and commitment. He or she should be thankful to God for their ability, but prayer did not magically accomplish it. I like basketball, baseball, and football, but frankly I don't believe God cares who wins a basketball or football game or a World Series. God may be concerned about what kind of sportsmanship you display on the field, and how you act while off of it, but I don't believe that God is primarily concerned about who wins or loses a game. With all the suffering, pain, agony, disease, and sin in the world, I don't believe that this is a major concern of God. I believe God is much more concerned about justice and righteousness in our relationships to others.

The Publican's Prayer

Look at the publican's prayer. The publican was not a well-liked person. He was considered by many Jews as the chief of sinners. He was working for the Roman government by collecting taxes from his own people and skimmed off the top whatever he could for himself. To the Jewish people, he was a traitor. He had become wealthy and fat off the money he got from his own people. He was seen as unclean by them because of his dealings with the Roman government. They didn't think he should even be allowed in the temple to worship. No Jew would go into his home. To go under his roof would make them unclean.

He Acknowledged His Sins

The publican lifted his voice to God and confessed his sin. He is deeply convicted of his sin. For some reason, he is aware that he has done wrong. He realized that he had hurt people, robbed them, and taken advantage of them. His gestures and prayers indicated his deep feelings of anguish. He beat upon his breast as a sign of his deep distress. There is no reference in the old Testament to people beating on their breasts like that. Usually this gesture was done by women in the New Testament. The publican is in such anguish of soul that he beats on his breast, maybe as a sign that he realizes that "out of the heart come the issues of life." He beats upon his heart that is breaking out of an awareness of his own sinfulness and his deep sense of guilt.

A Humble Man's Cry For Mercy

The tax collector has gone up to worship on the Day of Atonement. The cymbal sounds, the trumpets blast, the choir of the Levites sing, and the smoke of the incense rises into the air. As the atoning sacrifice is being made, he cries out: "Let it be for me, O God, let this atonement be for me, a sinner" That is the real meaning of his words, "Lord, have mercy on me, a sinner." "Let this act of atonement apply to me. Let me be forgiven." Here is a humble man's cry for mercy.

The doctrine of justification by faith did not originate with the Apostle Paul. Joachim Jeremias, the great New Testament scholar, states that this "passage shows that the Pauline doctrine of justification is rooted in the teaching of Jesus."[11]

Why Was The Publican Justified?

Jesus says this man went down to his house justified rather than the other. Why, you may ask? Why? The publican was aware that he was a sinner and he pleaded for God's mercy. His broken heart acknowledged his absolute dependence on God and not his own works. He realized his own inability to achieve his own righteousness. He depended utterly on God's atonement and mercy. He asked for God's forgiveness and acknowledged that forgiveness comes from God's grace.

The church was not established for the upright or the holy. If church people telegraph the message to others that only those who are okay can come to church or only those who have gotten their acts all together can come to church, we have misunderstood its reason for being. The church is a place for sinners. The publican was a sinner, who came to church, confessed his sin, and found forgiveness from God. He humbled himself and threw himself upon the mercy of God.

All Need God's Grace

Unfortunately, some people come to church week after week, year after year and never really experience the grace of God, because they think they don't need it. They assume that they are already right before God. God continuously reaches out to your life and my life with his grace and wants to lead us into deeper

---

[11] Joachim Jeremias, *Rediscovering the Parables* (New York: Charles Scribner's Sons, 1966), 112.

joy. God is always at work seeking to bring us redemption. You may have come to church for the first time today. You may even have come by accident. Maybe God's Spirit is saying to you, "My grace is sufficient. You can be forgiven of your sins and start anew." Maybe you have been coming to church for years and you have thought all along that everything was great in your life, and yet you know deep down inside your heart that something is radically wrong. God's grace can come into your life today and you can experience forgiveness. You can know that you are accepted by God and you are forgiven.

Don't base your religion just on your feelings. The Pharisee probably went home that day feeling that he was close to God. But he was wrong. The publican may have gone home that day feeling that he was a long way from God. Yet he was the one who was forgiven and justified. Religion is not just a matter of your feelings. We should rely upon God and not our emotions. Salvation is by God's grace. We respond to it and accept it.

Two men went up to the church to pray. Two men, plus women and young people continuously go up to the church to pray. One went down justified, forgiven. The other remained in his sin. Which one are you and I?

Trying To Make A Patch Do

(Parables of a New Patch on an Old Garment)

Luke 5:36-39

"Just who do you think you are?" they asked Jesus. "Just who do you think you are to break our traditions?" These were the kinds of questions Jesus began to receive. Too often, we have sentimentalized our picture of Jesus and think that everybody liked him, praised him, and wanted to make him king. We often forget the crucifixion. Mark's Gospel tells us that it was John the Baptist's disciples who began to ask Jesus that question: "Why do you break our traditions?" Matthew's Gospel records that it was Jesus' disciples themselves who asked him. In Luke's account, the Pharisees are the ones who asked him this question. Most likely, at one time or another, all of them asked Jesus why he had broken their traditions.

Jesus responded to these questions, as he often did, with a parable. In fact, he gave them two very brief parables. One parable was simply about a patch on a coat. This probably indicates the poor background of the home life of Jesus. He, like many of us, grew up watching his mother put patches on garments and understood that kind of story. The other parable about the wineskin was also a familiar picture. The Palestinians did not use glass bottles and plastic bottles had not been invented in which they could store wine. They used the skins of animals. In the two parables, Jesus describes the nature of religion, which he had come to place in our hearts.

We Hold Onto The Old

One of the lessons we can learn from these parables is this: Too often we want to cling to the old and familiar, and we will not give way to the new. I can understand that difficulty, and you can, too. We all often prefer the old, familiar pathways. We like the old haunts and familiar vacation spots. We enjoy the restaurants which we have been to, that are tried and true. We all somehow or another like, desire, and want the old familiar places.

I remember a few Christmases ago when I got a new pair of bedroom slippers. It took me a long time to get used to the new pair because the old ones were so much more comfortable. I could slip into them so much easier than the new pair. That is sometimes our problem also with new shoes. The old shoes are really more comfortable, though they may not look like they should be worn anymore. But we usually enjoy them more because they are more comfortable and more familiar. I, like many of you, enjoy antiques. I think one of the reasons why I like antiques is that I understand the traditions out of which they come. I feel confident about antique furniture being made of solid wood. I understand the heritage behind them. Their familiarity gives me a sense of safety and security.

Carlyle Marney told about a small boy who said to him one day: "Here I am seven years old and I really wished I was one-year-old." Dr. Marney asked, "Why?" The boy responded: "If I was one-year-old, I could bite somebody and they couldn't bite back." There is a kind of safety and security in knowing something like that. We all often prefer the security of knowing that at a point we can do something and it is okay, even if it is biting someone else. We know that at another stage in our life, it will not be okay.

Moving is one of the experiences which often shatters the lives of so many people. You come into a new community and have to face people whom you don't know, often being uprooted, and now you must find a new place to live. You are thrown into new surroundings, and have to start all over. Changing jobs can have a similar effect. For most people, that produces tremendous trauma and difficulty. We long instead for the familiar, the secure, the known, and that which we can handle without tension, frustration, or difficulty. Retirement can be a similar experience.

Some of us are a bit like the Arab native who one night lit a candle in the darkness of his tent. He reached over to get a fig, opened it up and noticed that it had worms in it, so he pitched it aside. He opened another one and noticed that it had worms in it and pitched it aside also. He did the same with the third. Thereupon he blew out the candle, and then reached over and got the fourth one and ate it.

Some of us, rather than face the unpleasant surrounding of a situation, simply had rather live in the darkness and go on. We prefer the familiar and secure rather than the unknown. But Jesus is telling us that this is not the kind of religion he is seeking to initiate. His religion comes as a disturbing force in the world. It is often revolutionary in its impact on our lives. It comes as a mighty disturbance to the status quo.

Harsh Words To The Religious

I think we need to understand that our religious traditions are often repugnant to the mind and spirit of God. Some of the harshest words Jesus ever spoke were leveled against the religious leaders. Note — not non-religious folks — but religious people. He said that some of the religious leaders had used ancient traditions in such a way that they placed them around the necks of people and these traditions had become a yoke that was crushing them to the ground and destroying them. The traditions had become like a millstone. "You are a generation of vipers." "You are whitewashed tombs," Jesus said. He declared that they were making it more difficult for people and not more liberating.

The More Significant Part Of The Law

The children of Israel believed that they were God's chosen people and they wanted to hold on to the past and their traditions. They continuously forgot that God had blessed them to bless others. God's blessing was not something they were just to keep for themselves. It was something that they were to share with others. They had tended to build a fence around their beliefs and their traditions. They had attempted to make their religion a closed system, and others were excluded. They began to teach that only those who were Jews could be the children of God. The laws, traditions, and interpretation of their relationship to God began to expand, and these soon became the weightier parts of what they emphasized in their religious practice. Jesus broke that way of thinking and challenged the whole legal system that the scribes and Pharisees had built and declared that they had chosen not the weightier part of the law, but the least essential and had lost that which was most important. Sometimes we commit the same kind of sin today.

We also seek to build our religion on our experience alone. "My experience with God is all I need," we think. So, we begin to build fences around that experience and exclude any other kind of new experiences that challenge us to new ways and new directions. We seem to declare: "The way I have experienced God is the way of coming to God." We begin to make our own experience the only way of approaching God or understanding who and what God is. Jesus is telling us in these parables that you can't contain God in the wineskins of old experiences, because God is constantly bursting them asunder with fresh insight, new breezes, open windows, open doors to bring new directions and new ways. God's spirit is always going before us and pulling us into new avenues of serving God in the world today.

Several years ago, when I was a speaker for young people at Ridgecrest, I had finished speaking that day and a woman came up to me after the service and said: "Did I hear you say that after a person has become a Christian he needs to continue having experiences with Christ?" "Yes, that's what I said," I replied. "You can't say that and be a Baptist," she asserted. "Who says I can't?" "I did and I am!" I responded. One of the very reasons I am a Baptist is because of the freedom we have to interpret the scriptures as one is led by God.

Continuous Spiritual Growth

The heresy which she was seeking to put on me is the heresy we see too often within many denominations today. This heresy is the view that all one needs to do to be a Christian is to say "yes" to Jesus one time and our spiritual growth is over and complete. There is no place in the New Testament where that is taught. The New Testament always speaks about new birth, new beginnings, new song, new commandment, and new life. Salvation is a place of newness. It is a place of new beginning, not a place of ending. The new birth indicates that one has become a new creature — a new creation by God. Following this experience, each of us is then growing, developing, and being nurtured by God. We should be spiritually deeper and more mature today than we were yesterday, or we have not really understood what it is to be Christian? The Christian life is a call to a life of growth and openness to the freshness and newness, which God has before us.

All change produces some pain. In fact, it is unlikely that any real growth takes place in our lives without some pain in it. Most growth comes about by change, and almost all of us resist change in one way or another. Jesus is telling us very clearly in these parables that he has come to give us the freshness and vigor of a new way of life which challenges us to move forward as God's people in the world.

The Need To Be Flexible

Secondly, Jesus also tells us in these two parables that we need to be flexible. In Palestine, wine was put in the skins of some animals like a goat. Then the skin was covered with pitch, and the neck was secured so the wine would not spill out. As the wine would ferment, the skin, being new, was flexible and would expand. The new skin could stand the strain caused by the wine. If one had an old skin which had become dry and someone put new wine into it and it began to ferment, of course, it would burst the skin and the wine would be lost. Jesus is saying that his gospel is the new wine. It could not be contained in the old skins of Judaism. He did not advocate that if one wanted to become a Christian, he or she must first become a Jew. His gospel exploded that old wineskin.

The Gospel Shatters Old Wineskins

Down through the centuries, the gospel has continued to shatter old wineskins. It burst the wineskin of slavery and declared that all people before God are free people. It burst the wineskin of segregation and declared that before God all people are one. His gospel continues to burst old wineskins that linger within us. This gospel will burst the wineskins which are trying to contain the rights of women today. It will one day burst that old wineskin so that women can have more freedom and equality with men in our day. It will burst the old wineskins of religious dogmatism and many others. It will break the old wineskins of provincial religion. It will break the old wineskins that try to limit our understanding of God to ancient Greek metaphysical systems. It is breaking the old wineskins which try to contain the way we speak about God or to God in some ancient language like the King James Version vocabulary.

When a new pastor is called to serve a congregation, the church must be open to new ways of ministry. As significant and fine as the pastors in the past have been, this church cannot keep its eyes on the ministers in the past. The church cannot remain confined to the old wineskins of the past, no matter how great they may have been. It must now look to the future and how God will work through the new pastor who will offer a new "wineskin" with fresh leadership.

God is constantly bursting these old wineskins and coming to us with the freshness, newness, and vitality of the divine presence. God is always the Creator, and God is still seeking to create us anew as individuals, God's people, and as a church. God is always calling us to become more than we are. No old skins can ever contain the freshness of God's spirit as it pervades our lives. Faith is always dynamic not static.

Change Is Often Met With Opposition

Change usually is met with opposition and difficulties. Who among us, if he or she is honest, would really want our medical doctors today to practice medicine like they did two hundred years ago? Did you know that almost every medical and scientific advance was met with continuous opposition? Galileo was banned as a heretic because of his scientific theories that the earth was not the center of the universe. Only in 1992, 350 years later, did the Catholic church acknowledge that it had erred. That is a rather slow response! Pasteur met opposition from other medical doctors when he encouraged them to wash their hands before surgery and when he tried to introduce some inoculations to ward off disease. Lister also faced stiff opposition when he tried to get other doctors to use antiseptic methods when they performed surgery. When James Simpson introduced chloroform, almost no one would use it.

Down through the centuries, many scientific and medical discoveries have been opposed by many in society. When the automobile first began to come down the road, people laughed and joked about that noisy contraption. Following the airplane's first flight, people ridiculed the Wright Brothers' efforts and thought that it would not amount to anything. Few papers thought that first flight important enough to carry an article on the event. Today you and I see the progress which has been made, in many areas, and every single one of us in some way or another utilizes these scientific advances and discoveries.

A Call for Openness in Religion

It is interesting that in the realm of religion we often remain more close-minded and archaic than in any other areas. This area ought to be the one where we are the most open to new truth. God, who is the Creator of life, is continuously opening us to freshness, vitality, new insights, and new direction. No one can ever say, "I have all the truth about God"; or "I have built a fence around God, and I know all about God"; or "I understand everything about the scriptures, and I know exactly how one can describe God"; or "Here are the ten theological tenets in which one understands what God is like." Blowing across the world are desires for changes in many areas. Jesus would remind us again about the God who cannot be contained in old wineskins, who is forever revealing the divine self with freshness and vitality.

A Gospel Of Joy

In the third place, Jesus is also telling us in this parable that the gospel is a gospel of joy. He responded in these parables to the criticism which some had directed against him when they accused him of drinking and eating too much with his friends.

"Why are you not more respectful in your religious practice?" "Why are you not sadder?" they seemed to ask. Jesus used the analogy of the bridegroom to tell them that while the bridegroom is present, rejoicing and feasting are the order of the day. The wine of his presence has burst the old wineskins and has given joy and invigoration. His gospel is volatile. It explodes old systems. It comes to us with a freshness, which is filled with joy and hope.

It is good news, and the good news is that we as individuals do not have to remain as we are, and we as a church do not have to remain as we are. God is constantly coming into our lives to reveal to us the possibility of newness for us as individuals and as a church. We do not have to remain in depression, or loneliness, or sin, or frustration, or anger, or indecisiveness as individuals. We do not have to remain divided with another or in controversy with other people. We can find the freshness of God's spirit, which brings God's love and grace into our lives, and transforms us to experience anew the joy of God's presence.

Jesus said, "I have come that you might have life and have it more abundantly." "I have come that your joy might be made full." Jesus said, "I have not come to destroy the law but to fulfill it." He fills it full with meaning. He has come to keep that which in the law is worth preserving. In the Shema, we read that "the Lord our God is one." Jesus attempted to preserve that which was old and worthy of saving.

A New Creation

Jesus also came to shatter the superficial and mundane. His work brought newness of life. Remember that Jesus Christ did not come simply to reform but to transform. He did not come simply to mend us but to remake us. He did not come simply to make some minor corrections but to bring about a new creation. We as individuals and as a church need to be a part of the new creation of God. That means, if we are the children of the new creation, the children of the new birth, the children of the new song, the children of the new commandment, the children of the new hope, we remain open and related to God's spirit which is continuously giving us new avenues for ministry, new opportunities for service, and new visions for acting and ministering as God's people.

Soren Kierkegaard was a noted Danish philosopher of the nineteenth century. He has an interesting parable about a preaching goose. A goose is probably a good analogy for a lot of preachers. In this parable, a goose is flying over a barnyard one day and notices that the dirty lot is filled with geese. He stops and gathers a crowd in the barnyard and begins to preach to them. He reminds the geese gathered before him in the barnyard of the adventures of their forefathers who flew the trackless skies in years past. He challenged them not to be content with their confined earthbound existence behind the wooden fence. He told them about the Creator who had made their life and had given them wings so they could migrate great distances. All this pleased the geese and they nodded their heads in approval. When he finished his sermon, all the geese applauded the sermon and spoke about the wonderful eloquence of the preaching goose. But they did not leave the barnyard. They returned to their corn and the security of the barnyard. They did not fly out of the barnyard. They remained there.

Lift Our Vision

God has called us as individuals to lift our vision beyond the immediate. God admonishes us to lift our vision to what we can become as God's people. There are always those who want to build fences around our visions and look down or look back. But God is calling us to look ahead — to look forward at what we can be. The gospel we received from Jesus is always fresh, new, and vital. Jesus challenges us to lift our wings and fly into new realms of service and creativity. "The challenge to the church," Alan Culpepper reminds us, "has always been to distinguish the wine from the wineskins and to be ready always to find new skins for the wine. Repeatedly, however, the church has fought to preserve the old wineskins."[12]

Jesus is giving you an opportunity to decide today. Do you want your religion merely to be a patch on an old religious

---

12 Alan Culpepper, "The Gospel of Luke," *The New Interpreter's Bible*, vol. IX (Nashville: Abingdon Press, 1995), 132.

garment of your own design or will you be open to the radically new grace he offers? Are you going to close your mind to God and assume you have already learned all you can from him or will you remain open and responsive to God however God comes into your life? Will you settle for religious tradition and clichés instead of a real, vital, and joyous faith? Why settle for the stale and mundane when Christ offers you new life and radiant joy? The choice is yours.

I hope that we shall choose to be open to God and not be old wineskins. Jesus has already told us what happens to the old wineskins — they are burst asunder by the new wine. Let's be open to him and the direction that he is seeking to take us. His call is to go forward. The choice is yours.

The End Of Privilege And The Invitation To Unlikely Guests

(Parable of the Great Feast)

Luke 14:7-24

It was a cold February morning. A man stood warming himself over the fire that was burning in a large trash barrel. You could tell by his clothes, which were tattered and worn, that he was a street beggar. Suddenly a well-dressed a man came up to the beggar and handed him a card. The vagabond looked at the man as he walked off and then looked down and read the card.

"You Are Cordially Invited
To Attend a Banquet
To Be Held
In the Home of John Goodfellow
Louisville, Kentucky
Friday, February 12, 2017
(Cars will pick you up at the Jefferson Street Chapel at 6 P.M.)"

After reading the card, the beggar continued to watch the well-dressed man as he walked down the street. He noticed that he stopped by a cripple who was selling pencils and handed him a card. He observed that as the man went on down the street farther that he stopped by a blind man who was also trying to sell something and gave him one of the cards. He watched the stranger as he continued to walk down the street passing out his cards.

In a few moments, the beggar quickly ran up to one of the other people who had gotten a card and asked: "What do you think about this? Could this be on the level?" "I don't know," the other man responded. "But it's a free meal and I'm going. We can get out of the cold. It may be some kind of trick, but I am going."

Friday night at a few minutes before six o'clock, a group of very interesting looking people gathered in the lobby of the Jefferson Street Chapel. The group was composed of street walkers, beggars, bums, alcoholics — the rejects of life, or so it would seem. After a few moments, three large limousines pulled up in front of the chapel. The men had never seen such big cars in their lives. The chauffeur opened the door and the guests got in. Then they were transported to a house the likes of which they had never seen before. The cars drove down the winding driveway until they pulled up in front of a large mansion. The door of the house opened and they were greeted by a friendly host who welcomed them. He led them to a table which had been carefully prepared for the evening meal. As they walked in, they gawked at the lovely house. They had never seen such thick carpet, expensive furnishings, lovely paintings, such everything!

None of them knew the host who sat at the head of the table. Then he said, "Before we eat, let me say the blessing." "Lord," he prayed, "we thank you that we can gather here for this meal. We thank you for these people who have come to eat. Lord, you know who they are, and you know their names and you know their needs, and I know you care for them and you love them. Bless them and us as we share together in this food. Amen." Then he said, "Dig in!" And they did!

For a while, the men and women were busy eating. After a few moments, someone began to ask questions. The blind man asked: "What does the host look like?" Conversation soon began to go around the table. The host didn't have to do much prodding to cut through their thin excuses for not wanting more to eat. When he noticed that somebody had cleaned his or her plate, he urged his butler to come in and offer them more. When they had finished the meal, they moved over into a room nearby where someone was playing on a piano by a roaring fire which was burning in the fireplace. They all began to sing old familiar songs. Some of these men and women had not sung songs in years. Finally, they began to sing a few familiar hymns, such as "Amazing Grace," and "The Old Rugged Cross."

After they finished singing, the host said, "You may wonder why I have invited you here tonight. I asked you to come here because I want you to know that God loves you. I know that what I have done tonight is a small gesture. But it is my way of saying to you that I care for you. I want to give you a New Testament tonight. I have marked some passages in it so that you can read them when you are lonely, hurting, and feel that nobody is interested in you. I also want you to know tonight that if you do not have a job and you would like to find one, that I will help you get one. If you want some help to overcome some kind of problem that you may be having, whatever it is in your life, I want you to know that I am willing to offer you support, encouragement, and help with whatever need there is in your life. Now, in a few moments a chauffeur will take you back to wherever it is that you will be sleeping tonight. If you don't have any place to sleep, you are welcome to stay here and spend the night with me. I want you to know that I am trying to extend to you something of the love that I think God has for you."

As the men and women slowly walked out of the door that night, one gripped the host's hand and said, "You have given me hope. I was thinking of committing suicide, but you have given me hope." A woman said, "I am going to take you up on that offer. I can beat this problem with alcohol. I am going to come back and see if you can't help me find someplace that can rid me of this problem." A man walked out and said, "I haven't worked for a long time. Nobody would give me a chance. I am coming back and I want you to help me get a job." The cars drove off and soon they were gone.

As far as I know, this story that I just told you did not happen. And it is unfortunate, isn't it? Because it would have been very Christlike.

A Celebrative Dinner

Jesus had been invited to a banquet, a community feast. While he was there, Jesus began to tell stories, as he often did. One of the stories he told them was about the people who had been invited to a banquet. Jesus began his story by reminding his listeners that God's kingdom is a banquet, a feast — a time of celebration. It is a sad commentary on the church that people often equate being a part of God's kingdom with dullness and boredom. We frequently say or hear expressions like, "Dull as a sermon," "boring as church," or something being "tame as a Sunday school picnic." All of these images in some way or another denote the paleness and grayness of the church.

Before C. S. Lewis became a Christian, he had been an agnostic for most of his life. When he wrote his autobiography, he titled it *Surprised By Joy*. He had to admit that he was startled to discover that the Christian faith was really alive with radiance and joy. Jesus said that God's kingdom is like being invited to a feast — a banquet — where there is fellowship, excitement, joy, and happiness. When the birth of Jesus was announced, the angel exclaimed: "Behold I bring you good tidings of great joy." Jesus said to his disciples, "I have come that you might have life, and have it more abundantly." "I have come that your joy might be made full." Unfortunately, some have identified religion as being primarily a burden, duty, obligation, sacrifice or a way of denial. They have forgotten that the psalmist exclaimed: "I was glad when they said unto me, let us go to the house of the Lord."

A preacher's son, as many small boys and girls, and sometimes even adults do during the sermon, had occupied his time by naming the row of lights which surrounded the arch over the pulpit where his father spoke. He had named each light in the arch for a book in the Bible. One Sunday he noticed that one of the lights had burned out. At lunch that day he said, "Daddy, do you know that Lamentations has gone out at the church?" His father said, "Well, amen! Let it go." And amen indeed. Let it go. The church was created to be the organization where people can experience the resounding joy that is a vital part of the life of a Christian.

While Jesus was telling his stories, one of the men at the banquet interrupted him and said, "Blessed are those who will eat in the kingdom of God when the Messiah comes." Others around said, "That is wonderful. I wish I had said that. Amen brother." But Jesus poked a hole in that pie-in-the-sky dream of a religion, which was off someplace in the future, when he told them another story. The story he told was to remind them that they were looking in the wrong place or direction. The feast was not sometime off in the future. But the one whose banquet they were waiting to celebrate was among them.

Invitations To The Feast

Jesus told them a story about a man who gave invitations to people in his community to come to his banquet. In ancient Israel, two invitations usually went to the people who were invited to a banquet. The first invitation informed them of the time and place. When they accepted the invitation, this meant that they would come to the banquet. The host was going to buy the food and get ready for the banquet based on those who said they would attend. When a person said, "I will come," he was making a solemn commitment to be present. There is an old Arab saying that a second refusal to an invitation for a meal was a declaration of war. They took eating a meal very seriously in ancient biblical times. When the messenger came back to these people the second time, it was not the first invitation to come for a meal, but an announcement that the food was ready. "Come now," they announced. "We are ready to eat." Sometimes it would take hours or days to get ready for such a banquet. The second time the servant came, he was simply announcing the time of the banquet.

Jesus declared that Israel had been given an invitation to be God's children. They had accepted his first invitation but now that the meal was ready, they had rejected God's invitation to come to his feast. The time for celebrating God's banquet was not in the future Jesus was saying. The time is in the present. The Messiah is here among you. Respond!

I heard about a middle school teacher who decided that she and the students were going to give a surprise birthday party for one of the pupils in the class. The teacher contacted the boy's mother and made certain that he would be home on the day of the party. A few minutes before the teacher and his classmates arrived, the boy's mother asked him to go outside and play for a while. The teacher and all of his friends came in and they got everything ready for the party. Then the mother called, "Johnny, Johnny come home." But Johnny didn't come. She called, called, and called. But she couldn't get Johnny to come. They went on and had the party anyway, even if the special guest wasn't present. Later that afternoon Johnny came in. His mother explained to him what had happened and asked where he had been. "Well, I went over to the school ground nearby and played. I heard you calling, but I thought you had some chore you wanted me to do. So, I didn't come."

God calls us. We hear his voice. But sometimes like this small boy we don't respond, because we think it is a call to something that we may not like. By not responding, we miss the party.

Excuses For Not Attending

Jesus stated that when these men received their invitation the second time, they all began to make excuses. The words in Greek mean that all of them began at the same time to give a barrage of excuses. All of the excuses are laughable. Jesus was making a point by using humor, and the ancient Israelites would have thought that these excuses were hilarious. We have become so stuffy in the way we read the scriptures that we can't see the humor. Jesus was poking fun at the shallow reasons people give for not responding to God's message. All of these responses were ludicrous, and nobody would have taken them seriously.

The first man declared, "I can't come. I have just bought a field, and I have to go look at it." The listeners would have burst into laughter. They knew that no Jewish man went to look at a field after it got dark. Nobody examined a field after he had bought it. He would survey every inch of that ground, check out every rock, cave, stump, tree, and detail in it before he would purchase it. It was an absolutely ridiculous excuse.

This man's excuse might be symbolic of the excuses we give in our business life for not doing what we need to do in God's kingdom. Our work comes first. We become so absorbed in our work that we can't begin to see any opportunity to serve God because of the demand of our work. Just as the field was more important to the man than the host, so many today put their business affairs before worship or service to God.

The second man said, "I can't come. I have just purchased five team of oxen and I have to go try them." They would have burst out laughing again. No Jewish man would ever have bought any animals, especially ten oxen without trying them out first. He certainly wouldn't go at night to test them. Oxen were usually purchased in the marketplace. A field near the marketplace was used to test the animals.

This excuse is almost like telling somebody, "Well, I'd like to come to dinner tonight, but I really can't. I have just spent $12,000 for a car, and I'm going downtown tonight to Joe's Used Car Lot to see what I have purchased. I hope it's okay." "Yeah, um huh," you would say to yourself. "I wonder if that person has rooms for rent!" Nobody does that kind of thing. What we have is a pretext — a rude affront. The oxen might represent our quest for novelty, our longing for power or production or pride in our possessions. But if they stand between us and God, our emphasis is misplaced.

The last excuse would have been even more laughable. "I can't come because I have just married a wife," the other man replied. No Jewish man ever used a woman as an excuse for anything. Men never mentioned women in public. No Jewish man did that. When Jesus used this as a man's reason for not coming to a banquet, they would have screamed with laughter. "What kind of man would ever say that?" they thought to themselves. All of these excuses, even those about family demanding first place, are wrong. Our family life is very important. But some parents have their children involved in little league, ballet, music lessons, and everything else and allow these things to crowd church, religion, and God out of their lives. If God and church are pushed out of your life, what kind of marriage or home do you really have? We become so busy with other things, even important other things, that God is left out of our lives. Of course, these other things are important. All of the things these men talked about were important in their proper place and time. When these things usurp the place of God first in your life, your priorities are misplaced. We are attracted to the second best and let the best slip away.

There is an old eastern story about a man who came to borrow a rope from a friend. The owner said, "I am sorry, but I cannot lend you the rope. I am tying up a heap of sand with it." The man who needed the rope said, "You can't tie up sand with a rope." "Oh, but you can," the owner said, "if you don't want to lend the rope to somebody."

Our Excuses Today

Excuses — all of the excuses by these men were laughable and ridiculous, and the people knew it. But so are ours. Listen to the excuses we make for not putting God first in our lives. We hear these excuses all the time, and unfortunately sometimes may use them. "I can't go to church. I'm… I'm just too tired. I need my rest." "I can't do anything in church. I just have to find time for my family." "I have to do this, or I have to do that." "I'm not going to church. I don't like the preacher." "I don't know those songs." "It's too hot." "It's too cold." "I don't know those people. They are not warm." We make excuses of all kinds. "They are not nice to me." "They hurt my feelings somewhere in the past." "I don't like that Sunday School teacher." "I don't like the way they are leading the church."

We hear and make all kinds of excuses. Why don't we just say it and be truthful. Our real problem is our own indifference to God. We let everything else crowd God out of our lives. We don't have our priorities right.

I will never forget a man who used to sit on the second pew in one of my congregations. He was there every Sunday. He never missed a Sunday. But now, you need to know Mr. Smith was stone deaf. He couldn't hear a freight train running through his ear. He couldn't hear a thing. Somebody asked him one time why he came to church when he couldn't hear anything. He said he came for two reasons. One, because it was his testimony to the importance of the church and worship, and secondly, he absorbed something about God from simply being there. If there has ever been anybody who had an excuse not to go to church, it was Mr. Smith. But he was there in church every week.

Remembering Your Earlier Commitment To God

Do you remember when you first made a promise that you were going to commit your life to God and follow and serve him? Do you remember that promise? Do you remember it? Think about it now! For some of you, you may have made that promise when you were a small child, a teenager, or as an adult. Some of you have made new promises recently to God. Are you keeping them? Are you beginning to let all kinds of excuses press those commitments out of your life? Are you beginning to settle for the second best in your life instead of seeking to put God as the first priority? Does your commitment to God affect everything in your life?

Several years ago, I was called to the hospital late one night. When I went to see the man who called me, I asked him why he had telephoned me. I didn't know him at all. "Well, to be honest with you," he said, "you were the only minister I could get who would come. I tried several others." I talked with him a while and discovered that he was frightened that he was going to die. He had never committed his life to Christ, and he didn't want to die without making that decision. We talked about that for some time. After a while, he opened up his life and committed it to Christ. He said he wanted to become a Christian and accept Christ, change his life, and serve him. I came back and saw him the next day and the day following. I invited him to church when he got well. But he never came. I have often wondered what happened to this man. When he was between the rock and the hard place and thought he was going to die, he made a commitment to God. I have wondered whether or not his commitment was real. When he got in the sunlight of day and began to go back into his normal pattern, I wonder if he remembered the promise that he had made to God and kept it. We often make promises to God and then permit excuses of all kinds to crowd these promises out of our lives. We reserve no place for him.

The Invitation Extends To All

Then Jesus said that the rejected host invited everyone to fill his empty table. The original guests were the leaders of Israel.

The lame and the poor of the city were the outcasts within the house of Israel. Invite those who are not considered orthodox to come to the feast. Then he told his servant to go into the highways and hedges — to the Gentiles — and invite them to come. The invitation to come to God's kingdom feast, Jesus says, extends to all people — the well, wealthy, religious and also to those who are the outcast, hurting, hungry, lame — sinners all. They are invited to come and experience the wideness of God's mercy and forgiving grace. God's banquet invitation is not extended to some special, select group of holy people. God invites all sinners to come experience his redemption and rejoice in the forgiveness which he provides. After all the people from the streets and lanes, highways, and hedges, have come, Jesus said, "There is still room."

Anthony Campolo, an American Baptist professor and teacher, told about an experience he had when he went to Honolulu to give a speech. He indicated, as you know, that there is a six-hour time difference between Honolulu and the east coast. He said he was wide awake at three o'clock in the morning and found himself hungry. He got up to see if he could find someplace to eat. He looked around and all that he could find was a greasy spoon. He sat down at the counter and ordered a doughnut and coffee. While he was drinking his coffee at three-thirty in the morning, several prostitutes walked in, and one sat down on one side of him and one on the other. Soon the whole little greasy spoon was filled up with street walkers. They were talking back and forth and the one on one side of him leaned over and said to the other one, "Hey, tomorrow is my birthday." "Big deal" the other said. "What do you want me to do 'throw a party for you?" "Naw, nobody has ever given a party for me," she said. "I have never gotten a birthday cake in my life."

After a while the prostitutes left. Campolo turned to the manager of the small restaurant and asked: "Do those women come in here every night?" "Yeah," he said. "Why don't we give this woman, what's her name?" Campolo asked. "Agnes," the man responded. "Why don't we give Agnes a birthday party?"

"Why that would be a great idea," the manager said. "I'll buy the cake," Campolo said. "No," Harry said, "I'll furnish the cake." "Okay, I'll come back tomorrow night," Campolo said.

The next night at two-thirty in the morning, Campolo arrived on the scene. He put streamers and crepe paper all over the place. They had a big cake ready, and a sign behind the counter which read: "Happy Birthday, Agnes." Campolo said that they must have gotten the word out, because every street walker in Honolulu was in that small place. At three-thirty Agnes came in. She walked in and saw the sign, "Happy Birthday, Agnes." Suddenly everybody began to sing, "Happy Birthday." Then they brought the cake out. She stood there frozen, unable to say a single word. She was spellbound. They asked her to sit down. "Cut the cake and give us some," someone said. "Cut the cake, Agnes." But she couldn't cut it. Harry reached over and started to cut the cake. Agnes said, "Don't cut the cake. Let me take the cake home. I've never gotten a birthday cake before. Don't cut it. Let me take it home." "Sure, that's fine," Harry said. Agnes took the cake in her arms and walked out of the door to go home.

Campolo said that there was absolute silence in the small restaurant. He said he didn't know what to do, so like a preacher he said, "Let us pray." He prayed for Agnes that she might come to know Christ, that her life might be different, and she might know God's love. After he finished praying, the manager leaned over and said, "You didn't tell us you were a preacher. What kind of church are you a member of?" Campolo looked back at the man and said, "I belong to a church that throws birthday parties for prostitutes at three-thirty in the morning." The man looked back at him without smiling and said: "Don't put me on, mister. I would love to belong to a church like that."

The good news today and every day is that Jesus Christ opens his arms to all people no matter where they are in life and invites them to come and experience the forgiving, loving, redeeming grace of God. This grace is extended not just to the righteous, but all people can come and find his redeeming grace. Come, experience God's love today. If you do not know God's grace, this experience is the greatest joy you can ever have.

Work: A Gift Of Trust

(Parable Of The Talents)

Matthew 25:14-30

If you work to the normal retirement age, are you aware that you will put in 125,000 hours working? That is a lot of time spent working! Some people love their work. They enjoy it. They are fulfilled, enriched by it, and find it meaningful. Others hate their work. It is drudgery, a bore, a burden, and frustrating to them. Some of us are like the man who once said, "Oh, I love work. I can sit and watch it all day long." Others are like the man whose new boss asked his former employer about him. "How long did Joe Smith work for you?" "He worked about four hours," his former boss replied. "I don't understand," his new employer said. "He told me he was with you for two years." "Yes," the old boss replied. "He was with us two years, but he worked only about four hours."

Some are like the tramp who stopped by a woman's house one day and asked if she had any work that he could do to earn some food. "I don't think," she said, "I have enough work to occupy you." "Madam," he responded. "You will never know what little work it takes to occupy me." Some of us take that kind of attitude toward our work. It is a burden to be borne, something to be endured, not something we really enjoy or feel is worthwhile. The Christian faith should have something to say to our work since it consumes so much of our time. If our religion does not address our workday life, then it misses a huge segment of our existence. I want us to look particularly at the parable of the talents, because I think it has a message regarding our work.

Biblical Meaning Of Talent

In biblical times, the talent was a weight and not a coin. The value of the talent was determined by whether the coinage used was gold, silver, or copper. In the Good News Version, talents are rendered as gold coins. If they were gold coins, it meant that they were very valuable, but they may have been silver or copper. The most common metal used was silver. An employer who was going to another country entrusted a separate amount of talent — money — with a certain value and opportunity of investment to each man. Let's see if there are some lessons for us in this story.

God's Gift To Us

Notice, first that each one is given his talents. The talents are bestowed upon them. They come as gifts. When we stop and think about it, all of our opportunities in life really come to us as gifts from God. The great worker of all workers is God. God is the master worker who has created the world and given life to us. God has given opportunities to you and to me that we might likewise work and labor with him. Work comes as God's gift to us.

I know there are some people who want to say that the third chapter of Genesis depicts work as a curse from God. If Adam had not sinned, we would not have to work, they suggest. When the scriptures are read carefully, especially the creation story in the first chapters of Genesis, we observe that God created man and placed him in the garden to tend it and care for it. Man was to be a worker before sin came into the world. We are to be coworkers with God. Sin has made our work more difficult, like it has made all of life more difficult, but work is a gift not a curse that comes to us from the great worker of all — God. Our first lesson is that work is bestowed by God. All work, opportunities, and talents come to us as gifts.

Differing Talents

Secondly, we observe that each one in the parable had differing talents. We don't have to look around very long before we know there are great varieties of gifts. Some people obviously have a whole lot more abilities than others. You and I have been in school with some individuals who seem to have all of the intellect that one could imagine. They can master any subject so quickly that it is threatening and intimidating to the rest of us.

I recall, when I was in high school, a student who was a couple of grades behind me, thank goodness, achieved the highest average anybody had ever achieved in our high school. Nobody ever saw Bobby Smith study. Maybe Bobby studied, but no one saw him bring his schoolbooks home. Bobby had a mind like a steel trap. Once he heard something; once he read it, it was there forever. He was just brilliant, but he intimidated his fellow students with his great brilliance. Now, the Bobby Smiths are rare in life. As we all know, not all students are like that. Most of us have to struggle, study, and work to acquire knowledge.

There are varieties of gifts and levels of intelligence. In this parable, we observe that one man had one talent, another two and still another ten. There was a variety in the gifts that they had. So, it is with all of us. We are not all ten-star individuals. We do not all stand at the pinnacle in everything that we have. In music, we are not all Bachs or Mozarts. When it comes to writing, we are not all like Shakespeare or Elizabeth Barrett Browning. When it comes to inventions, we are not all like Henry Ford or Edison. When it comes to sports, we are not all like Larry Bird, or Michael Jordan. In art, we cannot all paint like Michelangelo or Van Gogh. We may find that we have to struggle to express ourselves. Some of us have lesser abilities, while others seem to abound with talents and gifts.

One great thing about you is that you are an original. No one before you and no one after you is exactly like you. There are no carbon copies of you. You have gifts that have been bestowed upon you, gifts which God has entrusted to you. We do not all have the same opportunities. We may not all have the same advantages. Yet you have your gift to use in your time and your moments to the very best of your ability.

One of the fears I do not have when I stand before God is that he is going to ask me: "Bill Tuck, why were you not like Moses? Or why were you not like Paul? Why were you not like John Bunyan, or Fred Craddock?" He is going to ask me if I used the gifts he gave me to the very best of my time and ability. We all have a great variety of gifts. Don't be frustrated if your gift or gifts are not equal to someone else. In life, we sometimes find that the ten-star people are not always the individuals who make the greatest contributions. They may simply sit on the gifts that they have and not continue improving them.

The One Talent Man

Third, the main thrust of this parable, however, is upon the man who has only one talent. He is an interesting person. He doesn't seem to be an evil or dishonest person. He was not a thief; but he was unwilling to try. He did not do anything with the gift which he had. Why?

Afraid To Use Our Gifts

Well, one hint we have from the scripture is that this man was afraid. Fear is often a factor that keeps some people from using their gifts effectively. Sometimes they are afraid that they will be misunderstood, ridiculed, or judged harshly. We may not use our gifts because we are afraid of failure. We hold our gifts, opportunities, and abilities tightly to our breast, unwilling to try. We are not sure how others will receive us. So, we bury our gifts deep inside ourselves.

Routine Or Monotonous Work

This man, like many in our own day, may have thought that his gifts and talents were trivial, and the routine nature of his work seemed too unexciting. Some work in this man's age and our own is dull, monotonous, and routine. In our present age, many suffer more from work that is monotonous and trivial. The mechanization of society makes some people wonder what value their job can possibly have. All day long they sit at their work and turn one screw into an appliance and then another and then another. They may sew labels in the back of shirts all day long. Another may install brakes in one car after another. Another may put bumpers on all day long, or implant one tiny chip into a circuit. Many of these people become frustrated with the monotony of their jobs which seems to go on and on in their sameness.

A homemaker knows the unending routineness of taking care of a home. A house has to be cleaned constantly, and all the other responsibilities of a home are endless. A woman remarked once, "Cleaning a house is like threading pearls on a string without a knot at the end." Housework is never completed. There is a routineness about it that goes on and on and is never fully finalized.

In one of the "Peanuts" comic strips, it is still dark and Snoopy is sleeping on top of his doghouse, when Lucy comes by and says; "Wake up you, stupid beagle. It's five o'clock." He said, "Oh, no!" "If we're going to skate in the Christmas show," she said, "we've got to practice and practice and practice." He asked, "While the stars are still out?" "Stop complaining," she said. "Getting up early in the morning is good for you." "I hope so," he said, "because it's killing me!"

Some of our jobs with their routineness and constant demands seem to be killing us. They are taking us under. We want something that will be exciting and not routine that will break through the monotony. But we often forget that all of life has a certain amount of monotony, routine, and repetition in it. We are able to listen to Zollene, our church organist, plays the organ on Sundays because she practices weekly. She has put years in preparation before reaching this point of routine practice and study. Practice and study may sometimes get boring and monotonous. It is certainly routine. Our choir cannot perform effectively without practice and discipline.

It is awfully easy for us to look at a great athlete who seems to play so easily and forget the hours of practice and discipline that go into making him play as he does. The player who does the place kicking on a football team often is seen standing on the sidelines kicking the ball again and again into a netted backstop. An actress appears to do her part so naturally. She stands up before her audience and performs with ease. We forget the hours of study, getting up early for makeup and all the lines to be memorized. A doctor's job could never be monotonous, could it? He or she often follows a routine of rising early, seeing patients each day,

day after day, performing surgery today and performing another tomorrow. It is very demanding, and requires years of study, practice, skill, and discipline. Lawyers find that years of practice and discipline are essential, but much of their work is routine. Teachers walk into the same classroom day after day and have to live with a certain monotony. It is a part of life. We have to learn to live with that realization.

Our Gift May Be Insignificant

Some of us, though, have a hidden fear that our talent or ability seems so insignificant. This was a part of the problem with the man who only had one talent. "What was his one talent compared to the others who seemed to have so much more?" he thought. If there is any lesson which Jesus has taught us, it is the power of the seemingly insignificant. Jesus spoke about the significance of the widow's mite. He talked about giving a cup of cold water in his name. Small gifts given in his name become powerful instruments. Though small, think of the importance of a visit to someone in need, an embrace, a handshake, a telephone call, a word of concern. All of these are important. No task should be seen as insignificant.

A Higher Purpose Of Our Work

All jobs have significance when we see that each one has a higher purpose. A part of the problem with the man in the parable was that he had lost sight of the purpose of his gift. Many of us have not seen the higher purpose of our work. The man whose job is to put brake shoes in cars needs to remember the dependence others have on his workmanship when they drive their cars down the highway. Brakes have to be reliable. If the worker looks down the road to the person who drives the car and not just to that moment, then his job takes on more significance.

Workers who are building the tail section of large airplanes need to see their work as more than a monotonous day after day task; they have to see the importance that it has for the lives of more than three hundred people when they fly. These workers are doing something that is far more than just putting in a few frames in the tail section of a plane. They have the lives of hundreds of people in their hands. When our church building was being constructed, the bricklayers placed brick after brick on top of each other. That can be a very monotonous job, but, when one has a vision of a beautiful church, then his work takes on a greater significance.

A Vision Of The Greater Good

We need a vision and purpose to see beyond what we may be doing in our work at the moment and see the greater end, the greater good that we are doing for others. A woman, who was a homemaker, once said that she had learned to find a blessing even in the making of beds. As she made up the bed, she thanked God for the night's rest which she had. When she took out the garbage or cleaned the garbage can, she expressed thanksgiving that they lived in a society where they had so much that they had trash.

We need to see beyond our immediate task to envision the greater purpose in our daily work. If we lose sight of that higher end, our daily work may become only monotonous, routine, boring, and dull. When we see that we are co-creators, co-laborers with God, what we may be doing in this place, in this moment, in the plant, in the office is a part of the way we serve humanity.

All Gifts Come In Trust

Note fourthly in this parable, that all of the gifts come in trust. Each one of the men is given his gift as a steward. The gift is not to hoard, to keep, to hide, to bury in the ground, but to be used, and if we do not use them, we lose them. The man in this parable lost his gift when it was not used. This is a principle of life. If you do not use your gifts, you lose them. Maybe you could play the piano when you were young, and you have quit practicing. Try playing it now and you will see that since you have not worked at it, you have lost your gift. If you have ever studied a foreign language, you know that if you do not use it, it will leave you, and you will lose it. Many of the things we have in life come as a gift and must continuously be used.

When we were out west on vacation several years ago, we visited several deserted mining operations and saw numerous abandoned cabins. These structures had collapsed and trees and shrubs had begun to grow up through them because of their lack of use and attention. The wilderness had literally taken them over. Because they were unused, they had gone back to nature. This same principle is true in our own lives. We lose friends sometimes because we have not worked at the relationship and it has been lost. Our talents come to us as a gift from God, not to be hoarded, not to be put in the ground where they rot, but to be used.

Our Gifts Are To Honor God

Notice finally that all three of the men were given their talents to honor the master. All of our gifts were given to us that we might honor and praise God. All of our work should in some way be a part of our worship. Worship and work should be linked together. Meeting at eleven o'clock on Sunday morning is not the only way we can worship. Through our work, we express our worship of God.

A theologian once asked a man, "What Christian thing do you do?" "I bake bread," he responded. "No, no," the questioner asked: "What Christian thing do you do?" "I bake bread," he answered.

Your work can be one of the most significant avenues of ministry as a Christian. You serve God through your work whether it is a significant job by the world's standards or whether it is a small job. Every place of service is significant in the eyes of God, because you are a co-laborer with God. You can serve God as you help others in society.

It is interesting to me that God called Moses, not while he was sitting in a temple, but while he was tending sheep on a mountainside doing his daily task. Out of a burning bush, God called him to service. Jesus called Peter and John to come follow him while they were tending their nets as fishermen. Matthew was called from his tax collector's desk. Ananias was called while he was making ceramics to go and assist Paul, who had been blinded on the Damascus Road. Nehemiah was the cup maker for the Persian king, and he was called by God to go back and help rebuild the wall around the city of Jerusalem. Jesus spent most of his life as a carpenter. Only three years were devoted to his work as a preacher. In his work, he still glorified God.

In a small Moravian church, the congregation uses a workbench as their communion table. During the week, one of the men in the church uses it as his carpenter's workbench, but then, on Sunday it is brought into the church and used as the place where they commune and fellowship with God. Should not all of our work be like that? Through our work, we serve, minister, and worship in God's name.

For me, the fall of the year had always been a sort of a new year. I guess that is because I spent so many years in school, either working as a student or teaching, and found it a time of new beginning. On Labor Day weekend, for some, it is a time of going back to school. It is a new beginning of moving into a new community. Whether you are a teacher, you drive a bus, you do financial planning, you are an accountant, whether you are an attorney or a doctor, a carpenter, or a bricklayer, or student, let your work honor and glorify God. There is a great adventure in work when we realize that it is a medium where we worship and serve the great God of the universe.

Standing Up For Kindness

(Parable Of The Good Samaritan)

Luke 10:25-37

An American couple had planned for many years to go to Australia. Finally, they saved enough money to take the trip. They enjoyed visiting some of the larger cities like Melbourne, but they decided one day to visit a remote section in the back country. They rented a jeep and started down one of the roads. They had driven several hundred miles into the back country when suddenly their jeep began to sputter and finally stopped. The husband got out of the jeep to see if he could find out what was wrong. While he was working on the jeep, he noticed a car coming down the road toward him. "Ah," he thought, "maybe this is someone who can help us." But a man jumped out of the car with a gun in his hand and demanded all the money which he and his wife had. The American resisted at first, and when he did, the robbers began to beat him. They knocked him down, broke his arm, and left him lying wounded on the side of the road. They not only took their money but stole everything of any value which was in the jeep. He lie bleeding and hurt on the road, while his wife tried to give him whatever assistance she could.

Soon they saw a jeep approaching with several men in it. They recognized a noted American preacher. His face was seen every week on television. They knew they would get help now. The car pulled up, and the preacher asked them what had happened. They explained what their problem was. "I wish I could help," he said, "but I have a TV appearance in Melbourne, and I simply can't stop. If I do, I will be late. We will let somebody know you are here. We will call for help." And he rode on down the road.

Several hours later another car approached. This time it was a group of Baptist missionaries to Australia. They stopped and asked what had happened. The woman explained. One of the missionaries said, "I wish... I wish we could give you assistance, but we have to attend our annual missionary conference where we have to give a report of our work. If we don't get there in time to tell about what we are doing in our mission work here, our funds will be cut off. We must go on. We will let somebody know and send help back." They, too, went on down the road.

The sun was beginning to set and the wife was wringing her hands in desperation when suddenly another car came over the hill. This time a car stopped and a group of men got out. She could hear them speaking in a language that was unfamiliar to her. Then one of them, who could speak English, explained that he was a Russian. They were a group of Russian delegates who had come to Australia to arrange some cultural exchanges. Realizing the American was hurt, they came over and began to give assistance. They bandaged some of his wounds, placed a splint on his arm, and then lifted him into the car. They drove back to the nearest city, found a hospital, and explained to the doctors in the emergency room what had happened. "Whatever the cost is," they exclaimed, "we will pay for it." Then they drove off.

The story that I just told is, of course, fictitious. But do you get the point of it? Do you understand the reason you felt the way you did toward people who did not help this American couple, whom you thought should have helped, and the unexpected people who became the heroes? The parable which Jesus told two thousand years ago was probably even more dramatic than this story.

A Dramatic Parable

Jesus may have been sitting very close to or beside the Jericho Road when he told this parable. A crowd of people sat around him, listening as he taught. After Jesus had been teaching for a while, a man stood up, which was the customary way a student asked a question in that day of a teacher. He stood up to ask his question and also addressed Jesus as "Teacher," out of respect. Everybody knew immediately who this man was. All you had to do was to look at his robe. He wore a traditional lawyer's robe. They recognized him and were surprised that he would ask a question.

Around his forehead he wore a small calfskin box which was bound to his head with a leather thong. This small leather box was called a *phylactery*, which contained certain scripture quotations. It symbolized his orthodoxy. The box likely contained quotes from Deuteronomy 6:4-5 and Leviticus 19:18. "Hear, O Israel. The Lord is our God, and the Lord is one. Thou shalt love the Lord thy God with all thy heart, mind, soul, and spirit, and your neighbor as yourself." He touched the small box when he left in the morning and touched it when he came in at night. He was a lawyer of the Mosaic law — a religious scribe.

"Teacher," he asked Jesus. "What must I do to inherit eternal life?" Jesus looked at him and said, "It is right there," pointing to his phylactery. "You know the answer. Why are you asking me that kind of question? You already know. You are a scribe, a keeper of the law. You know the answer to your own question. What does the law say?" "The answer," Jesus was saying in essence, "is bound around your forehead and you repeat it each day. You shall love the Lord your God with all your heart, soul, mind, spirit, and your neighbor as yourself." Then Jesus noted, "You do this and you will live."

The lawyer knew that he had not communicated very clearly the question on his mind. He had not come across well. He realized that he of all people should have already known the answer to the question he asked. Trying to justify himself, he asked: "Who is my neighbor?" That question is familiar, isn't it? You know that lawyer, don't you? Yes, you know him. Why you see him all the time. Sometimes the lawyer is a banker, a carpenter, a doctor, a teacher, a secretary, a homemaker, or an accountant. You know this lawyer. You sometimes see him in the mirror. He or she is that person who thinks that religion is primarily for discussion. If you talk about religion enough, you have done it, he thinks. "Who is my neighbor?" he asked. He wanted to know the limitations of his neighborhood. What are the restrictions? How far do I have to go in being a neighbor? What is necessary to be respectable? What is my duty?

In response to that question, Jesus told a parable about a man who traveled from Jerusalem down the Jericho Road and was attacked by robbers and left bleeding and dying. Along this same road came a priest and a Levi. They passed on the other side. The Good Samaritan came along and gave him assistance.

Taking From Others

This story describes at least three attitudes toward life that I want you to note. The first attitude is "I'll take from others." This is the attitude of the robber. "I will take whatever I want. It doesn't make any difference who has it." The Jericho Road is about 22 miles long. When Jesus said the traveler went down from Jerusalem on the Jericho Road, that description is literally true. The road from Jerusalem to Jericho descends 35 hundred feet in those 22 miles. The road leads through rough terrain, with desert on both sides of the road which is intercepted with gorges and wadies. Robbers would often hide behind rocks and in the wadies along the way. This road has been called the "Bloody Way." Many people were often robbed along this road.

You and I know the robbers of life. They declare in veiled ways: "I will take whatever I want from you. It doesn't make any difference how it affects you or how it hurts you. I will get my way. You are simply a means to an end for me. I manipulate, abuse, use people, cheat, steal, or lie. It doesn't make any difference what happens to others as long as I get what I want. I will take from you and anybody else." This is a philosophy we see too often in life.

This attitude was illustrated some time ago in the comic strip, "Crock." Two soldiers are standing on a balcony overlooking a desert. A lieutenant spoke to his captain: "Sir, how do we know what's right and wrong in life?" The captain responded, "There's only a right and wrong if you get caught."

Too often, many follow this kind of philosophy through life. You do whatever you want to do as long as you can get by with it. It doesn't make any difference to you if you inflict hurt and pain on somebody else. That is irrelevant to you. Your selfish end goal is all that is important. The robbers did not mind giving pain to the man on the Jericho Road. They beat him and left him for dead. Many of those who inflict pain are unconcerned about their actions. You and I may be victims in life of their abuse. We simply get in their way, and they run over us or around us in any way they desire to get ahead or get their way. The pain we suffer may not be our fault at all. The robbers illustrate the attitude toward life of "I'll take from others."

Ignoring Others

A second attitude toward life reflected in this parable is: "I will ignore others." This is seen in the response of the priest and the Levi.

The Priest

Some scholars believe that the priest may have been going toward the temple to perform his religious duties. There were so many priests at that time in Israel that a priest only worked about two weeks a year in his official priestly duties in the temple. They were divided into 24 different units to perform their functions. If the priest was traveling toward the temple to do his two-week tour of duty there, he knew that he could be defiled if he touched this man who was lying by the road and he discovered that he was dead. To touch a corpse was one of the worst kinds of defilement that a Jewish person could experience. He couldn't take a chance and touch him. It might keep him from doing his sacred functions.

He also knew that the Jewish law decreed that whatever had happened to this man was the will of God. You know that attitude. We sometimes sing, "Que sera, sera — whatever will be will be." The fact that this man had been beaten and robbed was simply the will of God. He couldn't do anything to change that. God decreed it. He didn't want to be late for his official appointment in the temple.

But I am not so sure from a careful reading of the text that he was going toward Jerusalem. The text states that he was "going down" from Jerusalem. I think he had already done his priestly duty and was going home. He was in a hurry to be with his family. He was too busy to change his plans. Oh, he would have been defiled if he had touched the man and found out he was dead. But what difference would that make at this point? He was going home. He didn't have to do official duties now, and in seven days he would be clean anyway. He was simply rushing home to be with his family and did not want to take the time to be bothered with this man.

The Levi
The Levi was a holy person by heredity. He may have approached the man a little closer than the priest. He may have looked at his helpless form and heard his cries, but he went on his way as well. He and the priest passed on the other side. They were too busy; they had too much to do. "I'll just go on my way," each said. "I don't have time for this." They closed their eyes to the problems around them. They could say, "I didn't see you!" If you don't see, your conscience is clear. They thought that religion was more concerned with custom than charity, with being than doing, with seeing than assisting, with feeling than helping.

Helmut Thielicke, the prominent theologian and preacher in Hamburg, West Germany, told of an experience he had when he visited a well-to-do church councilman who invited him for tea one afternoon. In the course of the conversation, Thielicke expressed regret that part of the man's lovely house had been destroyed during the Second World War. Since then, it had been beautifully restored. "Don't talk about regret," the man said. "Even in this loss I experienced the grace of God." Thielicke said a warm feeling came inside him toward this man, and he thought how devout and humble the man is. But then the man finished. "God left me with just enough room so that I did not have to take in any refugees after the war." You see, his motive had not been right at all. It had been all wrong. "It had never occurred to him," Thielicke observed, "that the housing shortage had anything to do with one's relationship to God and our neighbor."[13] Although the

---

13 Helmut Thielicke, *The Trouble with the Church*, (New York: Harper & Row, 1965), 11.

man was devout, he did not see the ethical side of this particular issue. But he is not alone.

Our Own Images

The priest represents the noble citizens, the good folks in society, the church-going people, and the preachers. He probably told the man who was lying wounded in the ditch, "Friend, I am concerned about you. I want you to know that I hurt with you. I ache with you. I am sorry this has happened to you. As soon as I get home, I will organize a committee, and we will start a drive to clean up the Jericho Road." Oh, he had noble feelings and good thoughts toward this man. He may have even told him, "I will inform the Jerusalem Red Cross." "I will let the Jericho Salvation Army know of your plight." He was too busy with his own needs, concerns, family, and way of life. He was concerned, but he didn't do anything. He simply ignored him.

In Albert Camus' novel, *The Fall*, an attorney in Paris was taking a walk in a park one night by the River Seine. He passed a young woman who seemed to be in distress. A few moments later, he heard a splash in the river and a repeated cry for help. He felt an urge to run quickly and see if he could help her. The pull was strong to go help her. He heard her cry several times. But he did nothing and finally there was silence. Years have passed by and he cannot escape the memory of what happened that night. He is constantly plagued with what he did not do. One day in a confession, he exclaimed: "Oh, young woman, throw yourself into the water again so that I may a second time have the chance of saving both of us."[14]

Too often we just ignore people with their needs and hurts. We simply pass by on the other side.

Helping Others

There was also a third attitude in this story. It is expressed in the words, "I'll help others." Notice what an unlikely hero Jesus set before his listeners. A Samaritan! This was a despised person

---

14 Albert Camus, *The Fall and the Exile and the Kingdom*, (New York: The Modern Library, 1957), 147.

to the Jewish mind. This attitude of hatred had existed for four hundred and fifty years toward the Samaritans. In 720 BC when Samaria fell, some of the citizens were deported to Babylon, but not all of them. The Jews who remained there had intermarried with foreigners. These people were called Samaritans. They were considered half-breeds, a defiled people. When Jesus made the Samaritan a hero, the hair probably stood up on the back of the necks of his Jewish hearers. Their teeth were likely set on edge; their flesh may have begun to crawl. The Jews despised the Samaritans so much that they would take a day's journey longer to go another way rather than go through Samaria.

By Chance

Jesus said the Samaritan came that way "by chance." The word in Greek is better stated "coincidence." But the meaning contains more than our English word coincidence. The word is used in a religious sense of "coincidence" as though God was involved in that process of bringing the Samaritan near the certain man who was hurt. Seeing his need, he showed mercy. Mercy means "moving toward." He extended himself toward the wounded man in a deliberate act. He reached out to one in need. He saw a need and came to help. "Mercy is not traditional, not token, not sterile," Clarence Jordan wrote, "Mercy is the creative risk of unlimited involvement."[15]

Personal Involvement

Notice the personal involvement of the Good Samaritan in this situation. He went down into the ravine or desert area where the man was lying hurt and maybe unconscious. He touched him physically and began to bind up his wounds by pouring oil and wine on them to cleanse the cuts. This was the best medicine he had at that moment. He put himself at some personal risk by going to the side of the hurt stranger. Sometimes robbers used decoys to make a traveler think that somebody was hurt, and when someone tried to help them, they were attacked and

---

15 Clarence Jordan and Bill Lane Doulos, *Cotton Patch Parables of Liberation* (Scottsdale, Pennsylvania: Herald Press, 1976), 137.

robbed. He didn't know if the man was really hurt or was only lying there to entrap him. He also did not know whether this man had some kind of disease that he might catch. He could have been a leper. He did not know the real condition of the man. He exposed himself to some potential danger.

He placed the hurt man on his animal, and then took him to an inn. There was an inn about halfway down the Jericho Road from Jerusalem. Today, a hotel stands on the spot where some claim was the location of this ancient inn. The owner of the inn obviously knew the Samaritan. He may have been a businessman who traveled that way often and frequently spent the night at this inn. "Let me give you two denarii," the Samaritan said to the innkeeper. That may not sound like much money today, especially when you are aware that it was only forty cents in our money today. But in that day, it was the equivalent of two day's wages for a working man. "Take care of him," the Samaritan said, "and I will repay you any other costs he may run up on his bill." His repeated use of the personal pronoun "I" indicates that the innkeeper knew him. He was saying in effect, "You know me. I will repay you." The way the story is told, the Samaritan may have stayed up all night tending the hurt man's needs.

The Samaritan also made personal sacrifices to assist the wounded man. He most likely had business he needed to attend to, appointments with other business associates, wares to sell, places to be. He sacrificed his time, changed his schedule, and may have missed the next caravan going east and even lost a few sales.

The Possibility Of Being Misunderstood

The Samaritan also took the risk of being misunderstood by his Jewish neighbor. If the wounded man was a Jew, and it certainly seems evident in the story that he was, the fact that a Samaritan rescued a Jew might not sit well with the Jew who was rescued. He and his family might think that the Samaritan had defiled him by touching him. Kenneth Bailey, a noted New Testament scholar, observes that the Samaritan ran a grave risk of having the family of the wounded man think that he may have been the one who robbed him in the first place. If an American Plains Indian in 1875 brought a scalped cowboy into Dodge City on his horse and checked him into the local hotel, that Indian might be accused of being the one who scalped the cowboy in the first place. He could have a hard time convincing some of the other cowboys in that community that he wasn't the one who did it.[16] The Samaritan was so despised by the Jews that some might have assumed he had attacked the wounded man. The family of the victim might seek revenge on him. His act of kindness would not make any difference. He took a real risk. But Jesus said the Samaritan saw a need and went to meet it.

Who Is Our Neighbor?

Then Jesus turned to the lawyer and asked: "Who do you think then was the neighbor?" Notice that the lawyer cannot even say the word Samaritan. He doesn't say the Samaritan was the neighbor. He says, "The one who showed mercy."

Our Question Today

Who is your neighbor? That is your question and mine today. Where do you see yourself in this story? Identify yourself. Are you the victim? Are you wounded and hurting, waiting for somebody to come and tend your needs? Are you the robber or the priest? Or are you the one who shows kindness? As the story unfolds, we are actors in the drama, not merely observers.

The Importance Of Service

The test of religion is in service. The test of religion as Micah proclaimed is "to act justly, to love loyalty, to walk wisely before your God" (Micah 6:8 New English Bible). Jesus said, "You will know my disciples by their fruits." "Do unto others as you would have them do even also unto you." "Faith without works is dead," writes James. We can't just talk about religion. It must be seen in our lives.

D. T. Niles, the Indian minister from Ceylonese, tells the story about a man who was rushing through an alleyway and tripped

---

16 Kenneth E. Bailey, *Through Peasant Eyes*, (Grand Rapids: William B. Eerdmans Co., 1980), 52.

over a beggar. The beggar reached up and pleaded for help from him. The man looked at the beggar and said: "Friend, I would like to help you now, but I cannot. I have just become a Christian and I am rushing home to tell my family."

Sometimes we stumble across people in need in our pathway, and we do not even recognize them. Christian love is to be spontaneous. Wherever there are needs, we are challenged to reach out to help these people. Just like the father in the parable of the Prodigal Son showed extravagant love toward his son, God expects our love to be extravagant. Wherever there is need, let us respond lovingly.

Recognizing Our Neighbor

To ask the question, "who is my neighbor?" is the wrong question. That very question attempts to set limits. We are not to restrict who our neighbor is. To know who our neighbor is moves us beyond geography, countries, or space. To know your neighbor is not a concern for an area but with a spirit. Our neighbor is not determined by proximity but need. Our neighbor is not identifiable by fences but in opportunities for ministry. Our neighbor cannot be defined. There is an absence of limits. When we understand what it means to be a neighbor, we realize that all fences and walls are destroyed. All barriers disappear. All limitations are removed. We are neighbors to people of all races, creeds, skin colors, ranks, geography, or educational levels. God expects us to reach out to all human beings with love and compassion. Wherever there is need, we are challenged to respond in kindness and grace.

Dr. Jack Witten grew up in Tazewell County, Virginia. After graduating from The Medical College of Virginia, he decided to come back home to Tazewell to practice medicine. He had a disappointment in love and never got married. One night, Dr. Witten was ministering to a woman who was dying. She looked up at him a few moments before she died and asked, "Who will take care of my little boy?" Dr. Witten said, "Don't worry. I will." That began Dr. Witten's collection of boys. Over the years, 300 boys came into his home. Over 150 of them lived with him and many of them went to college. Wherever there was a need, Dr. Witten simply brought one of the boys into his home, loved him, cared for him, and provided for him. He saw a need and met it.

The Good Samaritan is symbolic of Jesus Christ and his ministry. Jesus' ministry is summarized in the compassion of the Samaritan. Jesus spent his ministry reaching out to people in need — to the blind, the deaf, the crippled, the lepers, the outcast, and the lost. He reached out with compassion to all people in their time of need.

The Jericho Road passes by your door every day. Its path may lead by the door at your home, at work, or the street you travel each day. Down the Jericho Road which passes your door, you encounter the hurting, the lonely, the wounded, and the needy that walk by every day. They reach out to you for help. Do you see them and hear them?

To Whom Am I Neighbor?

Who is your neighbor? That is not the right question. The right question is: "To whom am I neighbor?" Our neighbor is everyone who has need. "This parable of the Good Samaritan," A. T. Robertson wrote many years ago, "has built the world's hospitals and, if properly understood and practiced would remove race prejudice, national hatred, class jealousy, and war."[17]

A young man stopped one day to help a stranded motorist. As he got ready to leave after assisting the motorist, the man he helped asked: "What can I do to help you?" "As my father always told me," the young man replied, "whenever you see somebody else stranded, you stop and help them." "Who was his neighbor?" "The one who showed mercy," he replied. And Jesus said, "Go and do likewise."

---

17 A. T. Robertson, *Word Pictures in the New Testament Vol. 2*, (Nashville: Broadman Press, 1930), 155.

Emptiness Invites Unwanted Guests

(Parable of the Haunted House)

Matthew 12:43-45

When I was a boy, there was a big, old stone house several miles from where we lived. It had been abandoned for many years. Some of the windows in the old house had been broken out by vandals. Several friends and I loved to go over to the old place and play in the yard and in one room that was open because a wall had fallen down. Occasionally we would sneak inside through one of the partially open doors. Once inside, we noticed that the old, abandoned residence was filled with cobwebs, dirt, and clutter of all kinds. We would often see mice scampering around, and several small trees had pushed their way up through the floor. One night several of us decided to be very daring, and we slipped into the dark house. We pushed the door open and felt our way along as we walked slowly through the darkness. Suddenly we heard a sound upstairs, and the place became empty again! I don't know if that strange sound was just a few mice, bats, or an old tramp who had wandered in. We didn't hang around to find out!

We all know stories about houses that people say are haunted. When I worked in California one summer, I remember visiting an abandoned mining town. As I walked down the street, I noticed buildings of all kinds that lined the street. At one time, they had all been occupied, but now they were abandoned and stood empty. What at one time had been hotels, stores, offices, and businesses were all now standing empty, except for clutter, cobwebs, and desert animals or snakes. Tumbleweeds rolled down the street and sometimes into the deserted buildings. The rumor was that the town was haunted. Many people were afraid to come there at night, because they believed that ghosts from the desert nearby would come in and get you, if you were foolish enough to be there at night.

Jesus knew something about people's imaginations when it came to haunted houses. He lived in a day in which people thought demons were everywhere. People believed they lived under bushes, in the darkness, in the desert, in lonely places, and even inhabited people. Drawing on this belief, Jesus told a ghastly, chilling parable which grips our attention like an eerie, ghost story. His strange story focused on an old house which had been swept clean by its owner. The demon within had been cast out, but nothing had been put in its place, and it remained empty. This wandering demon saw that the house was empty and brought seven other demons with him to fill the empty place. Jesus said that the man's state was now worse than it was before.

The Ancient Fear Of Demons

What are we to make of this strange story which our Lord told? In Jesus' day, people saw demons everywhere. Today most people have difficulty believing in demons at all, at least in the way the ancient mind perceived them. The gospels show that Jesus himself did not accept many of the traditions about demonic forces. When someone asked Jesus, "Who sinned, Lord, that this man was blind?" Jesus did not attribute the man's blindness to sin or some demonic force. Jesus did not subscribe to the contemporary belief that demons inhabited fragments left over after meals. After the feeding of the five thousand, Jesus told his disciples, "Take up the fragments, save them." He didn't follow the restrictions of washing one's hands ceremoniously because of the fear that spirits might remain on unwashed hands. He did not believe in the tradition that demons resided in borrowed water. This is seen in his request of the Samaritan woman for a drink of water. He also did not ascribe to the belief that the desert was the favorite places of demons. He often withdrew to the desert to meditate and reflect. He would not have done that if he held such a belief.

Although Jesus did not subscribe completely to the traditional understanding about demons in his day, there is no question that the New Testament depicts Jesus at times exorcising demons from needy people, such as the man called Legion. How are we to understand this strange belief? Do we have to take this belief literally or could it have another meaning? Whether you take the exorcisms which Jesus did literally or symbolically, I believe they represent the awesome power of evil. Jesus is warning us about the terrible nature of evil. Evil is such a disruptive force in the lives of people that it can totally destroy their lives. He cautions his listeners to be alert in dealing realistically with the principalities and powers of darkness.

The Persistence Of Evil

What then does this parable of many centuries ago have to say to us today? I think that one of its messages is about the persistence of evil. The man had swept his house clean. He had driven the evil out. That was very admirable. He had gotten rid of the demonic force in his life, or so he thought. But he did not take into account the awfulness of evil. One does not battle evil once and it is over. It is a lifetime struggle. The story tells us that the demons were expelled — not destroyed. They were banished from his house for a few moments, but they were not totally obliterated. Evil is never completely overcome. The encounter with evil in our lives is a lifetime struggle.

Here is a businessman who has labored in his business for years. Honesty has always been his policy, we thought. Then we pick up the newspaper one day and discover that he has been arrested! What happened? He forgot that the struggle against evil is life-long. A politician may serve for thirty years, and then suddenly we read in the papers that he has been engaged in political corruption. Why? Because we sometimes forget that the struggle with corruption is not a one-time entanglement. It is a lifetime engagement. You may know a couple that has been married for thirty years. You hear one day that they are getting a divorce. Why? Because they forgot that marriage is not a relationship which is established one day and then each partner can take the other for granted. Marriage is a lifetime of mutual understanding, of giving and taking, growing, and developing.

Evil is never overcome in one broad sweep. Evil puts on new faces, new guises, and new disguises to confront us. Its apparel and appeal are not the same. Evil may be repulsed for a moment, but it has not been destroyed. It will raise its head up somewhere else. It awaits another moment, a new opportunity, a sundry occasion, or a different environment to meet us. Any individual who thinks that he or she has vanquished evil forever does not understand the awesome power of evil. We are constantly confronted by evil.

The Jewish people in Jesus' day thought they had vanquished idolatry. They had introduced many reforms into their religious practice. Israel had been swept clean of the false idols of Baal, Maleah, and the like. But Jesus indicated that Israel had begun to bind the hands and hearts of men and women with new shackles of idolatry which were worse than what they had before. Their rigid traditions of how one must wash his hands, observe the Sabbath, travel, dress, eat, do business, observe family life, and worship of God had become a new kind of idolatry. Jesus warned them against the new encroachment of evil which had come into their lives. They put their traditions and rituals before God's way. In refusing his message about God's kingdom, they had settled for a substitute religion which made them worse off.

The Lack Of Genuine Conversion

Jesus also warned against incomplete repentance or nominal conversion in his insistence on the persistence of evil. One of the worst heresies that we can tell a person is all that he or she needs to do is to come to Jesus Christ once! You and I will spend our whole lives battling evil. There needs to be a definite point of meeting Christ — a conversion, a transformation — but having met Christ at some point, then you need to be aware that you are challenged to a lifetime of growth. The Christian life is a pilgrimage of always seeking to become more like Christ. There are many who have been inoculated with a mild, superficial, artificial dose of religion, and they are never able then to respond to Christ's summons to take up their cross and follow him or to count the cost in following him. Too often the church has set the requirements of following Christ so low or what it means to be a member of his church that I'm not sure that Jesus would even recognize those who claim to be his followers.

Tennyson reminds us of the commitment the knights made in King Arthur's court when they took a vow to serve him.

By so straight vows to his own self,
That when they rose, knighted from
Kneeling, some were pale as at the
Passing of a ghost, some flushed,
And others dazed as one who wakes
Half blinded at the coming of a light.

These men were so committed to their king and so awed by what had happened in that moment that their lives were forever different.

When you and I meet Jesus Christ for the first time, our lives should be radically different. But in that encounter, remember that our Lord has cautioned us to count the cost and to be aware that we are engaged in a lifetime pilgrimage which thrusts us into a battle with the dreadful force of evil. Paul has warned us that we battle "against principalities and powers" (Romans 8:38). Never take the powers of evil for granted.

Can't Remain Neutral Against Evil

Go a step further with me in your thinking and see if you would not agree that this parable also warns us about the impossibility of remaining neutral. Jesus said that the house was swept empty, but nothing was put in the place of the evil which was removed. He found it empty. It is not enough just to remove evil from your life. Nobody is saying that this act is not good. We need to remove evil. But having removed falsity, dishonesty, corruption, and other kinds of evil, then your life needs to be filled with positive good. As long as your life remains empty, it will be filled with something. No life can really remain empty. An old, abandoned house may appear empty, but, if you look inside, you will find that it is not really empty. It is filled with cobwebs, clutter, mice, rats, snakes, and other things. If a house (your life or mine) is swept clean, and then left unoccupied, evil will return.

Life seems to abhor a vacuum. In fact, physics teaches us that it is very difficult to create a real vacuum. If you pour water out of a glass, the glass does not remain empty, but is immediately filled with air. You have probably tried this experiment. Fill a glass with water and put a stiff piece of paper over the mouth. Make sure that no air can get under your paper. Turn the glass upside down, and you discover that the water will not spill out. The water fills up the space, and air cannot get into the glass. Move the paper ever so slightly and out goes the water and in comes the air. When anything is empty, something else will enter it to occupy the empty space. Plow up a field and leave it vacant. It will not stay vacant long. If you sow nothing in the field, soon weeds will take over. A forest fire may rage through a woods, burning all the trees to the ground. Soon you will notice new life growing back. It is so difficult to have a vacuum, because something else always races to fill the empty space.

This is also true with life. I hear people say sometimes: "Oh, my life is so empty. I feel so useless." Life for them has become dull, useless, boring, or routine. Their favorite song is, "I'm busy doing nothing, working the whole day through." They have found no real purpose or meaning. They feel worthless.

I read about a man who visited the Bell Laboratories and noticed a small wooden box shaped like a casket on an executive's desk. He asked the man what that was. The man reached over and turned on a switch on the side of the box. The top of the box opened, a hand came up, turned around, and then reached over and turned off the switch. The hand then went back into the box. The purpose of this contraption was simply to turn itself off.

There are some who feel that life is like that — empty, vain, futile, and without any real purpose. When our lives are empty, we feel this way about life. Often, we do not recognize that we are empty containers, waiting to be filled by God. We are restless until we rest in him.

The Value Of Positive Goodness

As you look further at this parable, note that Jesus teaches us the importance of positive goodness. When you have removed negative things from your life, you need to fill your life with some positive good. The scribes and Pharisees did not commit the gross sins. They were not guilty of adultery, stealing, or murder. But they were guilty of a new kind of sin — self-righteousness, religious intolerance, selfishness, and contempt for others. They saw themselves as superior people to others. When life is based primarily on a negative religion of "don't do this," or "don't do that," or "thou shalt not do this," we have shifted into a different category of sin. I heard about a woman who said that she didn't believe that we should teach children the Ten Commandments. "They give people ideas," she said. Well, maybe there is some truth to that. If your life is based just on things you don't do, it does give people ideas. It gives them the idea that religion is nothing other than what you don't do.

A churchman had been after a man for a long time to join his church. Finally, he met him on the sidewalk one day, and the churchman continued his conversation and urged the man to join his church. "Now, I want you to join our church," he said. "Here is what you have to do if you want to be a member." He gave him a long list. The man read the list, and noticed that it was a list of things he could not do. The man, who had been walking his dog, looked at the churchman and observed: "See my dog here, he doesn't do anything on your list either. But that is not going to make him a Christian or a church member. What I would like to know is 'What are you for? What do you do?'"

When religion is based on negativism, it has not understood properly the spirit or teachings of Christ. In this parable, Jesus reminds us that we need to push out the evil, and fill its place with good. We overcome evil by being absorbed by a positive good. Righteousness is not just the absence of evil but the filling of your life with good. Paul wrote to the Roman church and instructed them, "Be not overcome of evil, but overcome evil with good" (Romans 12:21). "Be filled with all the fullness of God" (Ephesians 3:19). Having turned away from sinfulness, now fill your life with love, compassion, understanding, prayer, and deeds of kindness. It is not enough to stand up and say, "I am against evil." What are you for? It is not enough to flee the rule of Satan in your life. You have to come under the reign of God in your life. Negative forces are pushed out as goodness comes into your life and fills the vacuum they leave. Paul wrote, "It is no longer I but Christ who lives in me;" (Galatians 2:20).

A hundred and fifty years ago, a Scottish minister named Thomas Chalmers preached a sermon entitled, "The Expulsive Power of a New Affection." I share these lines with you from that sermon.

> The love of the world cannot be expunged by a mere demonstration of the world's worthlessness. But may it not be supplanted by the love of that which is more worthy than itself? The heart cannot be prevailed upon to part with the world, by a simple act of resignation. But may not the heart be prevailed upon to admit into its preference another, who shall subordinate the world, and bring it down from its wonted ascendency? ...The best way of casting out an impure affection is to admit a pure one; and by the love of what is good, to expel the love of what is evil.[18]

Christ comes into our life to give us the power to expel evil by bringing into our life goodness, holiness, love, and grace. We overcome evil as we are absorbed by good. A woman rented a jeep one day to do some heavy work. She drove it onto a beach and soon found herself mired down in the sand. The more she would spin the wheels, the deeper she got. Finally, she walked to a service station nearby to see if she could get a wrecker to come and pull her out of the sand. The owner said that he would come and show her that she really didn't need a wrecker. He walked back with her to where the jeep was mired in the sand. He pointed to the gearshift and showed her a lever she had not noticed. He explained to her that the jeep had a pulling gear. He showed her how to shift the jeep into that gear, and when she did the jeep came out of the sand immediately.

Our lives have a pulling gear that can get us out of the sands and entanglements of evil, sin, and corruption. This pulling gear

---

18 Thomas Chalmers, "The Expulsive Power of a New Affection," 20th *Centuries of Great Preaching*, vol. III, edited by Clyde E. Fant, Jr. and William M. Pinson (Waco, Texas: Word Books Publisher, 1971), 306, 311.

is the power of God. It is there within us. The inner power of God's presence can expel the forces of evil within us and fill our lives with grace and love. Paul reminds the Philippians in his letter: "And now, my friends, all that is true, all that is noble, all that is just and pure, all that is loveable and gracious, whatever is excellent and admirable — *fill all your thoughts with these things*" (Philippians 4:8).

Finding Forgiveness

(Parable of the Prodigal Son)

Luke 15: 11-32

Several years ago, when I was teaching at Southern Seminary, I received an invitation to preach one Sunday at the First Baptist Church in Knoxville, Tennessee. After arriving there by plane, I was met by one of the deacons of the church who drove me to the motel. He turned to me and remarked, "I hope you are not preaching on the prodigal son Sunday." "I'm not," I responded. "But why shouldn't I?" "The last three visiting preachers that we have had," he said, "have all preached on the prodigal son three Sundays in a row!"

I suppose the story of the prodigal son has been worn smooth in the telling of it so many times. In preparation for this sermon, I came to a decision. Sometime in the future, I would like to preach a series of sermons on the prodigal son. I concluded that it would be better to do that than to try and say all I wanted to in one sermon from the many lessons I have discovered in this story. Henri Nouwen did that in his remarkable book, *The Return of the Prodigal Son*. I still have not undertaken that venture. This parable has been called the greatest short story ever told. Some have described it as the "parable of all parables." Others have called it "the gospel in a nutshell."

"A certain man had two sons," Jesus began. But if you are a woman, do not feel that you are excluded. Jesus held this parable up like a mirror so all his listeners could see themselves in the reflected image. At some time or another, it is every person's story. There are at least five scenes in this moving story. Let's look at them.

The First Scene

The first scene depicts the younger son as he comes to his father and asks: "Give me." "Give me my portion of the estate," he implores. At the death of the father, the elder son legally received two-thirds of the estate and the younger son got one-third. Kenneth Bailey, who is Chairman of the Biblical Department at the Near Eastern School of Theology in Beirut, says that in his conversations with hundreds of people, he has found only two occasions where the request was made to receive a share of the estate while the father was still living. In the first case, the father dropped dead several months later from the shock of it! In the other case, the father disinherits the son for asking for such a thing.[19] The younger son's request is a grave insult to the father. What he is saying to his father in essence is: "I wish you were already dead so I could have now what is rightfully mine." It was a shocking request. The father would have been hurt and humiliated.

Jesus stated that the younger son left home alone. This indicates that he was most likely still single. He was probably no older than seventeen. A Jewish man in ancient times usually married between eighteen and twenty. His request for his share of his father's wealth was a demand that he be set free from the authority of his father. He naively assumed that if he had money, he would have freedom. He requested his father not only to make a division of the property but to make disposition of it immediately so he could have his share in money. I know of few people who can afford to take a third of their estate and give it to a son at a moment's notice. This action may likely have put the father in some financial jeopardy. Who knows what hardships the son may have caused the father by asking for his money as he did.

This kind of request by the younger son would have outraged the whole Jewish community in that day. They would be shocked by such a harsh request and would have turned against him. We

---

19 Kenneth E. Bailey, Poet and Peasant (Grand Rapids: William B. Eerdmans Co., 1976), 162.

do not know what their family life was like. Nothing was said of that. The son simply wanted to leave. He wanted to be able to do his own thing. He longed to have freedom and be his own man. He wanted to be in charge, to have his fling, and to go his own way. Lost in his own self-centeredness, he demanded liberty. "Give me …Give me freedom;" he cried. "Set me free. Let me have my way," In his heart, he was already in the far country.

One of the amazing features of this story is that, although fathers were all powerful then, the father granted his son's request. He sold some of his property and gave the money to his son. Then he stood, I am sure and watched sadly, as his son turned and walked away from home. Can you imagine the thoughts which must have gone through the father's mind as he saw his son walk away? "What will happen to him?" "Can he take care of himself?" "Give me," the son had asked and received.

The Second Scene
The second scene shifts to the far country where the son began to be in want. We do not know where the far country was. Maybe it was Jerusalem or Babylon. We simply do not know. The far country for every age is different. Maybe the far country today is New York City, Las Vegas, or Atlanta. Who knows? It can be any place where one goes to live in a riotous way. "The far country," Augustine wrote, "is forgetfulness of God." He went to the far country and soon found that he had spent all. Friends surrounded him as long as he picked up the check. When his life focused on eating, drinking, and being merry, he was surrounded by friends and companions. This was true as long as he paid the way. There is no indication in the story that the younger son invested his money or sought to do anything worthwhile with it. Jesus said that he wasted it in riotous living. He threw it away foolishly.

Then a famine came in the land, and he was in want. Desperate for work, he tried to get a job with a local farmer. According to polite Eastern traditions, he offered the prodigal son a job feeding pigs which he knew he would refuse. He simply didn't want to fool with this Jew. But to his surprise, this Jewish lad accepted the job of feeding the pigs! You could almost hear the sense of shock that would go through the crowd of people as they heard that. A Jewish man feeding pigs! Unheard of! Pigs were unclean animals. The fact that he was tending pigs most likely indicated that he was not keeping the traditions and laws of his religion. These were of no concern to him now. During the famine, he could not find food to eat. He could not feed off the pods which the pigs ate. Some of the pods, called carob which the pigs ate in that country, human beings could eat. But these pods were most likely the wild carobs, which were bitter. Human beings could not eat them but animals could. During a severe famine, these wild carob pods were most likely all they had to feed the pigs.

The young man began to be in want. "And no one gave him anything." Oh, he had so many dreams. "Freedom! My freedom will enable me to do whatever I want to do!" he had dreamed. He thought he would have freedom, but he was enslaved instead, He thought he would find happiness, but he experienced sorrow. He thought he would find good things, but he only found the bad. He thought he would find life, but he only found death. He longed for happiness but discovered sorrow. He wanted plenty but found famine instead. His dreams were scattered. He had reached for his happiness like a boy reaching for a butterfly. When he had the butterfly in his hand, he thought he had it in his grasp. When he opened his hand, he saw only a smear. If you seek to find the meaningful life in riotous living, you will discover that it is an illusion which eludes your grasp.

The young man soon began to be in want, need or waste. He wasted his time. He wasted his mind. He wasted his body and he wasted his money. Worst of all, he wasted his life. Too many of us live like that. Our sin is that we simply waste our life away.

The Third Scene

In the third scene, the picture changes some. The young lad "came to himself." The word that is used here in Greek is really a medical term. Luke, the physician, described the response as a person who has "awakened" from a fainting spell. He came to himself and began to ask: "What am I doing? Who am I anyway?" We often say, "I wasn't really myself when I said that." "I was just out of my head when I did that." "I have found myself pulled in every direction." "I am trying to get myself together." "I was all to pieces." He had not known who he really was. At one time, he thought he had been himself, but now he began to realize that he had not been his real self. Before, he had exclaimed, "I gotta be me." But he had not seen himself at his best. We are told that "he came to himself."

One of the most vivid descriptions of the paradox of human nature is found in the words of Carl Sandburg's "The Wilderness." In this powerful poem, Sandburg depicts our human struggle with our divided nature through the various "animals in us that strive to direct our life. There's the wolf, the fox, a hog, a fish, a baboon, an eagle, a mockingbird — We are indeed "A zoo", a "wilderness." He concludes by saying: "I — got a zoo, I got a menagerie, inside my ribs, under my bony head, under my red-valve heart — and I got something else: it is a man-child heart, a woman-child heart: it is a father and mother and lover: it came from God-Knows-Where: it is going to God-Knows-Where — For I am the keeper of the zoo: I say yes and no: I sin and kill and work: I am a pal of the world: I came from the wilderness."[20] If we are honest, we all struggle with "the taint of self-interest" and our wilderness personality, which acknowledges that we are disposed toward selfishness, arrogance, greed, envy, hostility, prejudice, lust, and other sins.

Some people do not come out of the wilderness. They perish in the far country. In Alan Paton's beautifully moving novel, *Cry The Beloved Country*, the black African minister Stephen Kumalo had just visited his son who is in prison because of murder. His son was to be electrocuted soon. After talking with his son and noting that he was unrepentant for what he had done, an anguished cry arose from Kumalo's lips as he talked with a fellow minister:

> *He is a stranger. I cannot touch him, I cannot reach him. I see no shame in him, no pity for those he has hurt. Tears come out of his eyes, but it seems that he weeps only for himself, not for his wickedness, but for his danger.*

20 Carl Sandburg, "The Wilderness," in Cornhuskers (New York: Holt, Rinehart, and Winston, 1946).

The man cried out, can a person lose all sense of evil? A boy, brought up as he was brought up? I see only his pity for himself, he who has made two children fatherless.[21]

There are some people in the far country who never come to themselves. But fortunately, this young man came to himself. Why? We are not certain. Maybe he came to himself because he remembered his father. When he was in the midst of famine, he remembered the teachings of his father and he recalled the good life at home. His father's love was still in his memory. He became homesick. Famine caused him to remember, and his thoughts turned toward home again.

When he came to himself, he began to confess his sin. He cried out: "I have sinned against God and my father. I will arise and go home and ask to be made a hired servant." Do you notice that he doesn't say, "I will tell my father that my friends made me do it."? Or "My home life is responsible for it." Or "Television or my smart phone caused me to do it." Or "It is the books that I read." Or "It is the movies I saw." "The crowd around me caused me to get in this fix." "It was the circumstances I got caught in." "It just happened." "It is my nature," Or "It was caused by heredity," No, that is not what he says. What does he say? "I have sinned." He took responsibility for his own actions. "I have sinned." He offers no excuses; but repents. He acknowledged that his sin not only hurt himself, but it hurt his father. It had disgraced his whole family. His sin not only affected his father, his family, and himself, but he had also sinned against God. "I have sinned against heaven," he said. Then he said, "I will arise." He didn't say "I will stay in my sin and keep on doing whatever I have been doing." Instead he declared: "I will arise and go home." He leaves the far country and goes toward home.

The Fourth Scene

Then the scene changes again. Sin was not the final word. This time, the young son returned to his father. The story states that while the son was a long way off, his father saw him coming.

---

21 Alan Paton, *Cry the Beloved Country* (New York: Charles Scribner's Sons, 1948), 109.

How could the father see the son coming when he was a long way off? Why, it is obvious. He was watching for him! Can you imagine the mornings, the afternoons, or the nights when the father would go to the edge of his property and look longingly down the road for his son to come home?

John Watson wrote a delightful Scottish novel titled *Beside The Bonnie Brier Bush*. The novel tells the story about a stern old Calvinist elder named Lachlan Campbell. He kept everybody's theology straight in the glen, including the minister. He sat in judgment on his preaching to make sure that he did not say anything heretical or deviate from the awful sovereignty of God. He was so stern and rigid that finally his daughter Flora rebelled and left home. Campbell was so outraged that during the next meeting of the church session, he moved with his own lips that her name be stricken from the church roll.

He had always called God Jehovah, but gradually he learned to call him Father. His rigid attitude began to change. He wrote a letter to Flora urging her to come home and assuring her of his forgiveness. Thinking she would return at night, each night he lit a lamp and set it in the window so Flora could see her way home. "And every night till Flora returned, its light shone down the steep path that ascended to her home, like the divine love from the open door of our Father's house."

In this story God is seen as a Father who stands at the door and waits for his children to come home. God is a father who loves us. I don't know what image of God you may have. You may see God as a warrior, king, judge, Creator, first cause, divine mover, ground of being, or author of an infallible book. In this parable and other teachings of Jesus, God is seen as Father. Out of compassionate concern, God waits longingly for his children to come home again and be embraced by his love. When the father met his son, he didn't say to him: "What have you done with all of my money? Look at the mess you have made of your life. You look awful. What have you done to yourself?"

Can you imagine what the son must have looked like? He had been living during a famine in a pigsty. But the father embraced his son, and in Greek, the words declare that he continually kissed him. By kissing his son, his father showed him that he was reconciled again. The father instructed his servants, "Bring the best robe." The best robe had to be the father's robe. Putting the father's robe on the son telegraphed a message to the community that he was accepted as a son again. "Put a ring on his finger," the father stated. This ring was a sign of his authority in the family, "Put shoes on his feet." Only slaves went barefooted. He was a son, not a slave. The instruction to "kill the fatted calf" was an invitation for the whole community to come to a feast. A fatted calf was too much for a family. That would be a waste. This feast was for the community. The community had seen the father's disgrace, and now they are all invited to rejoice in the return of the son.

Why do we hesitate to come to God?

God waits for us with open arms to love us, embrace us, and kiss us. Come home. Just as the prodigal's father ran to meet his son who had been lost, God, our Father, comes to meet the sinner and welcome him or her home. He came all the way to calvary to express his love to us. Through his redeeming love, he kisses our past sins away, robes us in his righteousness, places the ring of acceptance into his family on our finger, puts the shoes of sonship on our feet, and proclaims a feast of rejoicing at our return. This parable vibrates with the joy in the heart of the penitent who returns home and the joy of a forgiving God when one of his children is reinstated. The convert begins his or her life in a joyful reception by the Father.

The Final Scene

Ah, if this story had only ended at the return of the younger son, we would all feel better, wouldn't we? But there is a fifth and final scene in this drama. In this scene, the elder brother enters the story. The elder brother hears music and laughter off in the distance. I don't know why someone had not gone to the field and told him about his brother's return. When he discovered what the festivities were all about, he refused to go in the house and remained outside. This is another insult to his father. It was customary for the elder son to mingle with the guests and entertain them. He was supposed to be responsible for making sure that the party went well. He, like the younger son, had now insulted his father.

When the father went outside to talk with his elder son, notice what his son said. "All of these years I have worked for you, and you wouldn't even give me a goat. I have kept all of the laws and traditions. But this son of yours, who lived with harlots, has now come back after wasting your money and you give him a great feast." What was he saying to his father? One of the things he reveals is that he is ungrateful. He had only worked out of a sense of duty. He did not express any real love for his father and what he had at home. "Son, you are always with me, and everything I have is yours." He was not thankful for what he had — his food, home, job, or fellowship with his father. He was unable to see that everything he had come as a gift to him and not because he deserved it. Rob Bell says the father in this parable redefines "fairness." "Grace and generosity aren't fair," Bell notes, "that's their very essence… The younger son doesn't deserve a party — that's the point of the party. That's how things work in the father's world. Profound unfairness."[22] Grace does not depend upon works and right behavior. God does not give us what we deserve, but responds out of unconditional love.

The elder brother was also unforgiving. "This son of yours," he says. He does not say, "My brother." He was unwilling to forgive his brother and accept him back into the family.

He was self-righteous. "I have kept all of the traditions. I have not transgressed any of your rules. I have served you for these many years." Even at a person's best, no one can make that claim. No one is without fault or free of sin. Although he had served his father faithfully through the years, his motive was certainly not proper.

He also revealed a religious life which was unattractive. Christian love should draw people to Christ and not repel them.

---

22 Rob Bell, *Love Wins: A Book about Heaven, Hell, and the Fate of Every Person Who Ever Lived* (New York: Harper One, 2011), 168.

Suppose the younger son had met his older brother at the door instead of the father. Can you imagine what kind of greeting he would have gotten? He would probably have turned and walked away. Henri Nouwen asked the question, "Can the elder son in me come home? Can I be found as the younger son was found?" He noted the difficulty: "How can I return home when I am caught in jealousy, when I am imprisoned in obedience and duty lived out in slavery? It is clear that alone, by myself, I cannot find myself."[23]

But you see, that is where this parable is directed to many of us. We can't put its message off by saying that it was directed primarily at the scribes and Pharisees in Jesus' day. We are the new scribes and Pharisees. We are the religious people today. Some of us have great difficulty understanding how God can be concerned about the outcasts in society, such as the criminals, the homosexuals with AIDs, hobos, bums, and bag ladies — the rejects of our society. These people haven't kept all of our religious and national laws. We view ourselves as better than these, and we are unable to see our own sin.

The father spoke tenderly to his son, who was also a prodigal, "Oh, my son," literally 'my boy,' "everything that I have has always been yours. Let us rejoice that your brother;" note his use of 'your brother', "has come home. He was lost, but he has been found."

I think, I believe, I *know* from the teachings of the scriptures that you and I will be shocked one day at the extravagant love of God. God is not stingy or narrow in his love. His love reaches out to embrace people whom many would reject. This parable is striving to help us see that ultimately, we are not to remain as the prodigal son or the elder brother, but as Henri Nouwen noted, "we are called to be the father" — loving and forgiving.[24]

E. Stanley Jones told of a young woman who ran away from home and went to a big city. There she ended up in a house of prostitution. Her mother heard what had happened and went to

---

23 Henri J. M. Nouwen, *The Return of the Prodigal Son* (New York: Doubleday, 1992), 76.
24 Ibid, 120ff.

look for her. In each of the houses she visited, she left a photograph of herself on the mantelpiece. One day her daughter came into the house of prostitution where she was staying and saw a picture on the mantel at a distance. Curiosity drew her toward it, and when she got close to it, she recognized that it was a picture of her mother. On the picture were written the words, "Come home." Signed, "Mother." She immediately left and returned home for a happy reunion that night.

In this parable, we have a picture of God as he extends his hands and says, "Come home. Come home." You can be like the elder brother and stay outside and claim to be self-righteous and lose God's love. You can remain outside his love and live like a servant and not be a son or a daughter. You can remain a slave to sin and not be his daughter or son. But he says, "Come home." Come home and experience God's forgiveness and grace. His love reaches out toward all of us. Whether you are a sinner in the far country or a sinner at home, you can experience the grace of God. Come rejoice in God's joyful love.

On Being Ready

(Parable of the Wise and Foolish Bridesmaids)

Matthew 25: 1-13

In ancient Palestine, there were usually three steps toward marriage. First, a couple would become engaged. Usually the parents transacted this engagement, often when the couple were children and likely had never met. The second stage was betrothal. The betrothal was celebrated with a feast and a special ceremony. The couple would then wait a year before the marriage ceremony would take place. Betrothal was a high time in the couple's lives and was considered so binding that, if the future husband died, the young woman would be called a widow.

The Marriage Party

This parable in the gospel of Matthew describes a part of the marriage ceremony which is the third stage leading to marriage. A couple in ancient Palestine did not go off to celebrate their honeymoon when they were married. They observed a week's festivities at home and were treated as a king and queen. A special banquet was given in their honor on their wedding night. This was the banquet that the young women in the parable were waiting to attend. With their lamps, they would go before the bridegroom and bride as they went to the marriage feast. No one was allowed on the street at night without some kind of lamp. They didn't have electric streetlights as we have today, so each person had to provide his or her own light.

The lamps that the bridesmaids carried looked something like small gravy boats. They were made of brass and filled with oil with the wick extended through the spout of the vessel. The lamp would often be attached to a pole. The pole would have a sharp point on the end and could be stuck in the ground while the young women waited for the coming of the bridegroom.

It was customary for the bridegroom to keep the wedding party guessing when he was going to arrive. That was just a part of the gaiety of the occasion. "When will the bridegroom come?" they would ask as they dozed. Since they were used to going to bed early in the east, it was difficult to stay awake. The bridegroom usually sent a runner ahead of him to let the guests know that he was coming. This would give them a chance to get up and meet him on the road. As the hour grew later and later while they waited for the coming of the bridegroom, the lamps of the bridesmaids consumed their oil since they had to continue burning all the time. Five of the young women had not brought additional oil with them, in case they used up what they had in their lamps. When the runner announced that the bridegroom was coming, the foolish maidens discovered that their wicks had gone out. "Let us borrow some of your oil," they said to the other five young women. "No, I am sorry. We don't have enough for both of us," they replied. "If we let you have some, then we won't have enough. Go buy some."

Well, you can imagine the trouble they had in ancient Palestine trying to find oil at that time of night. While they were looking for oil, the bridegroom came. The young women who had oil in their lamps joined in the festivities at the banquet to celebrate the marriage. The person who was chosen to guard the door was most likely not a member of the immediate family. He may have been someone they hired for the occasion. The "foolish bridesmaids" rushed to the door late and exclaimed: "We want to go in. We are part of the wedding party." "I am sorry, I don't know you," he responded. He was there to keep folks from crashing the party after a certain hour. He knew everybody would claim to be a "special" guest. Once the door was closed, it didn't make any difference who came. It was too late. Those outside could hear the party going on, but they could not go in after the door had been shut.

The Kingdom Was At Hand

This may seem like a strange story to us today, especially as we try to see what its message is for us. Many have interpreted this parable primarily as a prophecy about the second coming of Jesus Christ. Many sermons have been preached on this text, warning the listener to be prepared for the second coming of Christ. But I do not think that was the original intent of this story. The original purpose of the parable focused on the first coming of Jesus Christ. As the chosen people, the Jews should have been prepared for his coming, but they were not ready. They had not expected this kind of Messiah. The kingdom of heaven was at hand, but they were not ready for it, though the prophets had foretold its coming centuries before. They were looking for another kind of messiah. Were they looking for a messiah who would be robed in royalty, pomp, and military power? John the Baptist had prophesied that he was preparing the way for the kingdom. Nevertheless, when Jesus came, the Jewish people were not prepared for his kind of kingdom.

A Time Of Joy

This parable also tells us that the coming of the Christ was to be a time of great joy. A wedding feast was an occasion of festivity. The coming of Jesus as the bridegroom was to be a time of celebration. Jesus said, "I have come that you might have life and have it more abundantly." "These things have I spoken to you that my joy may be in you, and that your joy may be made full" (John 15: 11). Pope Francis remindeds the church that "the joy of the gospel fills the hearts and lives of all who encounter Jesus," and "those who accept his offer of salvation are set free from sin, sorrow, inner emptiness, and loneliness. With Christ joy is constantly born anew."[25]

A Time Of Waiting

This parable also reminds us that we spend a lot of time waiting. For centuries, Israel had waited for the coming of the Messiah. When he finally came, their waiting was over, but they were unprepared. We all spend so much of our life waiting. We wait to go to school, wait to finish school, wait to get married, wait for children to come, wait to get out of the service, wait to retire,

---

25 Pope Francis, *The Joy of the Gospel: Evangelii Gaudium* (New York: Image, 2013), 203.

waiting to do this thing or another. Much of life is spent waiting. Have we learned to live creatively in our time of waiting? How do you live "in the meanwhile" as life gets so daily?

The Women In This Story

Look at the young women in the parable. All of them had good intentions. They were all evidently known well by the bride and bridegroom, maybe good friends, or relatives. They were probably asked to lead the procession. They were dressed for the occasion. They had their small lamps prepared for this wedding. They were attentive as they waited along the side of the road. They all fell asleep as the night grew late — the wise maids as well as the foolish. There is no word here of condemnation because they fell asleep. They all did that. What was the problem?

They Were Negligent

When the bridegroom appeared on the scene, the foolish bridesmaids were simply not prepared for his coming. They heard the announcement, "Behold, the bridegroom!" But they were not ready. Why were they not prepared? Well, for one thing, they were simply negligent. They didn't do anything intentionally wrong. They had not deliberately done something to hurt or offend the bridegroom so they could not come to the wedding party. They fell asleep and did not bring enough oil to last late into the night. They are called foolish because they were unprepared.

Some of the problems we have in life come about simply because we do nothing. We are negligent. We may not do anything deliberately wrong, but by doing nothing we reap a harvest we are unprepared to meet. At times, I have had a fish tank in our den at home or in my study. I may love those fish. But I discovered that one of the ways I might ruin my fish tank and kill the fish in it was simply through negligence. If I chose to do nothing — never fed them, never cleaned the tank, never made sure the filter worked properly, and never changed the water, what would happen? Eventually, of course, the fish would die, and the fish tank would turn into a scummy mess.

We see what is happening to our rivers, lakes, air, forest, cities, and other things in life, because we simply do nothing. Negligence can be very costly. Industries pour raw sewage into our rivers and streams, pollute our air, and poison our food, and usually we do nothing. Our negligence will slowly take its toll.

Some Things Cannot Be Replenished

The references by Jesus to the oil in the lamps which is used up reminds us that there are certain things in our lives that are being used up and need to be replenished. Some people have the mistaken notion that their first encounter with Jesus Christ is all they ever need in their spiritual life. That was the beginning point. One of the worst heresies any church or denomination can teach is that the conversion experience is the end of one's Christian experience. Conversion is the beginning of our spiritual life, not the end. This experience challenges us to a lifetime of being open to God, to grow, develop, to be nourished and nurtured in the faith. No one's spiritual life is ever finished; it should be developing and growing through the years.

Do you know why some people are so unspiritual? It is just negligence. They do nothing to nurture their spiritual life. They do not worship or read the Bible. They never read any literature to help develop the spiritual life. They never attend Sunday school or a study group. They simply do nothing to work at nurturing their faith and wonder why their spiritual life is so barren.

A pastor called on one of his church members whom he had never seen in his church, though he had been a minister there for ten years. He had been told that this brother had not been in church as far as some people knew for thirty years. He went by to see if he could persuade him to come to church. "I don't need to come to church," he said. "I made a profession of faith. I had a religious experience." He named the year and date. "I have a baptismal certificate that says when I was converted. I have had a religious experience." The minister attempted to share with him the importance of developing his spiritual life by coming to church and being faithful in worship. Finally, the unfaithful church member said to his wife, "Go up to the attic and bring down that baptismal certificate that has on it the date of my religious experience." His wife went upstairs and in a few moments, she came back and stated: "Honey, I hate to tell you, but the rats have eaten up your religious experience!"

There are an awful lot of people whose religious experience has simply disappeared out of negligence. They have done nothing to nurture it. The oil from their lamp has gone out. One of the choruses I remember singing in youth groups was: "Give me oil in my lamp. Keep me burning. Give me oil in my lamp, I pray. Give me oil in my lamp until the break of day." We can't exist on just one tiny drop of oil called our religious experience. That experience should be replenished repeatedly. By remaining in fellowship with God, we grow and develop.

Oil is often used in the scriptures as a symbol of one's relationship with God. Prophets were often spoken of as being "anointed" by God to show the divine influence on their lives. Jesus himself claimed, "The Spirit of the Lord is upon me because he has 'anointed' me." Oil in this parable may well have been a symbol of the new power which Jesus, the bridegroom, gave to enlighten his followers.

Delay As A Sign Of Grace

Push deeper into this parable and notice some of the truths here about watchfulness. I am convinced that the delay of the bridegroom may be an indication of the grace of God. God delayed the coming of his son. Israel waited centuries for the coming of Christ. We wait and continue to wait for the fulfillment of God's coming in judgment upon us. His delay is a sign of grace. Listen to Isaiah's words: "Yet the Lord is waiting to show you his favor, yet he yearns to have pity on you, for the Lord is a God of justice. Happy are those who wait for him!" (Isaiah 32: 18).

The Opportunity May Be Missed

The parable clearly indicates to us that the opportunity to respond to God may not come again. The door was shut. The foolish bridesmaids could not go in. We always think we have more time to respond in life. "I will put my decision off," someone says. "I will make my decision about God, life, and other things some other time." But many of our experiences or decisions in life, if we do not use the opportunities when they come to us, may be gone, and we may never be able to recover them again.

You and I as adults cannot go back and recover our childhood. It is gone. If we are adults, we can no longer recover our youth. I cannot go back and be twenty or thirty or forty again. Those years are behind me. If I misused them or abused them or wasted them, they are gone. Nevertheless, I can use the time I have now, but the opportunities of the past are no longer available. We live too often with the mistaken notion that we always will have plenty of time. "And the door was shut." These are words of tragic sadness which indicate that there does come a moment when it is too late to respond.

There is an old story about the ancient sibyl who offered King Tarquin nine books that she said contained all the wisdom of the world. She asked a fabulous sum of money for them. He refused to pay it. On hearing his words, she retired and burned three of them. She came back before the king, and this time offered him the six for the same price. Again, his advisers told him to refuse. She retired and burned three more. She then came back and asked the same price for the remaining three. His advisers said, "Take them quickly before they, too, are burned."

Some of the opportunities that come to us in life, if we do not respond to them when they come our way, we do not get another chance to use them. They cannot be recovered. The door was shut, and the young women could not go in. Their opportunity to respond to the bridegroom was now past. They had wasted that moment. The exclusion was final. It could not be offered again.

Some Things Cannot Be Borrowed

Notice further that there are some things that cannot be borrowed. If you and I had told this parable, we probably would have given it a different ending. Our version might sound like this: The news that the bridegroom was coming was announced. The five foolish bridesmaids said, "Why our lamps are gone out! We don't have enough oil. Would you, would you let us borrow some of yours?" they asked the five wise bridesmaids. "Oh, certainly, we will gladly let you have some of our oil," the wise bridesmaids said. So, they shared their oil with the foolish maidens. In a few moments the bridegroom comes by, and they tell him what they have done. "I am pleased that you have shared with one another," he responds. "Send ahead," he said to some friends, "and get some more oil so everyone can have enough to come to my wedding feast."

That sounds like Jesus, doesn't it? It reminds us of other stories and teachings which he delivered. But this parable is not about forgiveness or sharing. This is not the story of the prodigal son or the lost sheep. This parable is not about love and grace. This parable is about being prepared, being ready, lest opportunities come and we miss them. Although the refusal of the wise maidens may sound harsh and unkind to us, if the wise young women had shared their oil with the foolish bridesmaids, they would not have had enough for themselves. Their lamps would have gone out, and none of them would have gone into the celebration.

Faith Cannot Be Borrowed

What is the message of this parable? You cannot borrow somebody else's faith. You cannot borrow the faith of your mother or father, brother or sister, son or daughter, friend, or relative. Faith must be your own. When you come to a great crisis in your life, such as a time of grief, if you have no personal faith to sustain you in those moments, you cannot borrow it from someone else. You must have your own. When you come to your own time of dying, you cannot borrow somebody else's faith. It must be your own.

When Mary of Orange was dying, her chaplain came in and tried to share the way of salvation with her. She looked up at him from her dying bed and said, "I have not left this matter to this hour." She prepared for it years before. When you come to your own time of death, I trust your faith will be personal so it will enable you to withstand the terror of dying.

Valuable Qualities Cannot Be Borrowed

You also cannot borrow somebody else's integrity, character, or courage when you come to your time of testing. When temptations or difficulties come into your life and confront you, you are cast back upon yourself and your own resources. You cannot borrow from another in that moment. Those occasions are your time to stand and be tested to see if the fiber of your being can withstand the storms that beat upon you. Traits of character are not transferable. You have to build worthwhile qualities into your own inner person.

A teenager told his father that some of his friends had urged him to join them in the bullying of a new student from a foreign country at school. He said that he felt that this was wrong and told his friends why. They laughed at him and started to ridicule him and called him a "wimp". He said that he was surprised and hurt by their response and asked his father if he thought he had done the right thing. His father assured him that he had indeed taken the higher moral road, and he was proud of him. He reminded his son that standing for what is right sometimes may be costly, but it is the Christlike way.

You cannot borrow character, integrity, and courage from somebody else. Begin now to develop your own. Inner character is not formed in an instant. It takes a lifetime. When emergencies break in on your life, you need not dread them. If the inner person has been growing more Christlike, you will come out stronger, not weaker. But not all fare well in the testing of a moment. "I have noticed that destiny in every case," Voltaire once observed, "depends upon the act of a moment." How you act in that moment of testing will depend on what your character is like within. In that moment, you cannot borrow what you may need. The resources have to be within.

Faithfulness Is The Key

The parable calls us to faithfulness. There can be no real spiritual growth without faithfulness. We often hear of people who join the church with a burst of enthusiasm. They are so excited about Christ and his church. "Oh, it's all so wonderful" they exclaim. "I have given my life to Jesus. My life has been changed." Then, in a few months, or a few years, their wick begins to grow dim. Their attendance at church is less frequent and soon they quit coming to church altogether. They soon fade into the background. They started with a great flourish, but they petered out, dropped off by the sidelines, and grew weary in the faith.

In the fall of the year, believe it or not, I actually enjoy splitting wood. To me, it is very therapeutic. I sometimes ask myself as I work away at a large log, "Which blow of the axe actually splits the log?" Is it the first one? No, it may not split with only one blow. Is it then the second, third, or fourth or however many it takes to split the log? The answer is that it requires *all* of them. Each blow, one after the other, splits the log. I work until the log is split. Every blow to the final one is important.

Your spiritual life is not made up of just one response to Jesus Christ. He requires faithfulness. Jesus said, "He that endures to the end shall be saved" (Matthew 10:22). To be faithful, you have to replenish the oil continuously in your lamp. Your spiritual life has to be a growing and developing experience and not be based on one emotional experience which you may have experienced somewhere in the past, as wonderful as that may have been. Faithfulness requires a vital relationship with God today.

Northwestern University is in Evansville, Illinois, on the shore of Lake Michigan. A bronze plaque was placed on one of the buildings on the campus in honor of Edward W. Spencer. Many years ago, there was a shipwreck on Lake Michigan, and several people were drowning. Edward Spencer, who was a student at the university, heard the cries for help and swam out into the water sixteen times to reach the drowning victims. He single-handedly rescued seventeen people. Finally, he fell exhausted on the shore and someone heard him gasping, "Did I do my best? Did I do my best?"

God doesn't expect you to be like everybody else. He doesn't expect you always to be the number one in your class, to be the best in your community, or to have the greatest gifts. There may be somebody who is smarter, brighter, more gifted, and more creative, but he asks you to be faithful with the gifts that you have and to do your best with them. You are challenged to let your lamp burn brightly so others can see the light of Christ's presence in you, and let it draw them not to you, but to Christ.

A Word Of Judgment

This parable is also about judgment. It clearly has a ring of finality about it. Three of the harshest statements found in the New Testament are located here. "Our lamps have gone out." "The door was shut." "I know you not." The judgment was unequivocal and irreversible. Borrowed religion was not possible in this moment. God gives us a lifetime of opportunities to respond. Although God is loving and graceful, there is the stormy north side of God's judgment which does not wink at sin and say that it doesn't make any difference what we do. God's judgment is real.

God gives us many opportunities to respond. But rather than responding to divine grace, we often procrastinate. The word procrastinate comes from two words, "pro" meaning forward and "eras" which means the morrow. We often put forward what we need to do now to some tomorrow. We unfortunately think that we have all the time in the world to decide our relationship with God. But we do not have endless opportunities to decide. At some point, the door will be shut. We are to be ready, to be prepared for the judgment which will come. There will be a time when the opportunity to respond has passed. "This is the day which the Lord has made." "Choose this day whom you will serve." Jesus said, "Come unto me all who are heavy laden and I will give you rest." "This is eternal life to know the son." "Seek the Lord while he may be found."

Seek Christ, come to him before the door is shut. He invites you and me to come and participate in the joy of his kingdom. The decision is yours. You can decide to go in and celebrate the joyful festivities with the bridegroom or remain outside the door, shut out of the kingdom of God. The decision is up to you and me.

A Reason For Living

(Parable of the Barren Fig Tree)

Luke 13: 6-9

Two thousand years ago, Jesus was asked the same question that many people raise today, "Why do good people suffer bad tidings?" While some faithful Jewish people were engaged in worship, Roman soldiers killed them. "Why?" the people asked. Jesus did not give a simple response to that question, because he knew there was none. He reminded them that the Tower of Siloam fell on eighteen Jewish people and killed them. He in no way blamed God for these things, but simply cut through the pain of their question and indicated that suffering was a part of the reality of life. But he used these occasions as an opportunity to warn them. "Unless you repent," he said, "you as a nation in a like manner will perish." In a few years the Jewish temple was destroyed and Roman soldiers killed hundreds of Jews. Some of them died in the temple while they were worshiping. Jesus held up a warning flag for the Jewish people and declared: "You are being given a second chance. You have an opportunity to respond to God's messenger and turn to him and repent,"

In ancient Palestine, the fig tree was one of the most prominent trees. It often stood as a figure for the blessing of the land in the Bible. "The fig tree's literal presence as a blessing or its absence as a curse," Bernard Scott informed us, "allows it to function as a metaphor for blessings and curses."[26] Jesus told a brief parable about a man who had a fig tree that was not producing. He was getting ready to cut it down when his gardener said, "Wait! Let's spare it. Let me put some manure around it and see if it will produce next year." The owner said, "We will give the tree one

---

26 Bernard Brandon Scott, *Hear Then the Parables: A Commentary on the Parables of Jesus* (Minneapolis: Fortress Press, 1989), 332.

more chance." Jesus was saying to the Jewish nation that God was giving them another chance — opportunity — to respond and repent. It was a parable about judgment and opportunity. Listen to its message for us today.

A Reason For Living

This parable teaches that everything has a reason for living. The purpose for the fig tree was to produce figs. That was its reason for existing. In this parable, the fig tree was symbolic of the nation Israel. The vine was often used as a symbol for Israel. Their purpose as God's chosen people was not just to receive his grace, but they were challenged to share this knowledge with all nations. But they were not doing that. They were attempting to hoard the goodness of God and keep this knowledge to themselves.

Sometimes today we hear people voice similar questions as those asked of Jesus. "What have I done to deserve this?" "Why do I have this kind of pain?" "What did I do to offend God?" "What sin have I committed that this thing has happened to me, or to my child, or to my family?" Sometimes in despair, people look out on life and ask: "What's the point of it all?" They can find no purpose or meaning in life. Their attitude is reflected in the note which was found in a nursing home after a woman committed suicide. "I am tired of buttoning and unbuttoning." Some people see no reason for living. They are at a dead-end.

The scriptures declare that all people have been created as children of God, and we are challenged to reach for the highest potential we can be as people. Jesus said, "Be ye therefore perfect as your heavenly Father is perfect." Reach to be like God. "You have been created," the psalmist said, "a little lower than angels — literally, a little less than God. Jesus said, "Seek first the kingdom of God." He has challenged us to reach for the stars, the impossible ideal, the unreachable star, and for the highest possibilities we have within us. Our reason for living is not realized in selfishness, but in giving our life to some cause beyond ourselves which will outlast us. We seek to open our life to God and what he wants us to do with our lives.

A story that came out of World War I told about a young soldier who was badly wounded and horribly disfigured in one of the battles. When he realized his predicament, he became bitter and longed to be dead. A plastic surgeon examined him and said he would restore his face if he could have a picture. He did not have a picture, and he was too depressed to care. "It doesn't matter, Doc," he said. "Well, I was never much to look at anyway before I was wounded. Suppose you just make me like that picture on the wall." The picture happened to be a portrait of Christ. The surgeon did follow that picture as his model. After the bandages were removed and the man looked in a mirror, he saw a face different from the one he had been familiar with before. His face bore a resemblance to the picture of Christ which had been on the wall. "Since I look like him," the soldier said, "there is but one thing to do — I must become like him."

The scriptures tell us that we have been created in the image of God. Having been made in his image, our reason for living is to be like God. We do not live for ourselves alone. In everything we do, let us attempt to live so we will glorify God.

Living A Useful Life

This parable also tells us that we are to live a useful life. The fig tree was of no value. It was absolutely useless to the farmer. The tree had taken up space for three years, but had not produced any figs.

Normally, a fig tree produced figs within about two years. The owner had already given it an additional year to produce. It made no difference to the owner that the tree produced leaves and gave some shade. The tree was not fulfilling its purpose for being in the garden. It was useless. As a nation, God had designated Israel to carry the message of his love to the other nations of the world. But they tried to hoard God's salvation for themselves. In a way similar to the fig tree, Israel was useless in God's mission.

A Hindrance To Life

The parable also indicated that the tree had become a hindrance. It was taking up space in the garden which other fruit-bearing trees could have. Water was very scarce in Palestine. All the water which was absorbed by a tree that was not producing figs meant that the trees which could bear figs were losing that water. That tree simply took up space but produced no fruit. Like this tree, our lives are not to be spent in seeing what we can get from life, but in seeing what we can give. Our goal is not to see what others can do for us, but what we can do in service for God.

The parable makes it clear that the uselessness of the tree will lead to its destruction. Since the tree produced no figs, it was worthless. In the end, it would finally be cut down and removed. This picture is true to life. If we do not use what we have, we lose it. If we do not exercise our muscles, they become weaker. If we do not exercise our mind, it will not develop. If we do not exercise our spiritual life, develop, and nurture it, gradually it wanes away. If we do not work at our relationships with other people, we will see them slowly slip away from us. Every person in God's kingdom has the responsibility of being useful. Each of us in his or her way is a minister for God. Every person is not asked to do something spectacular with her or his life. But each of us can serve in a quiet, simple way and contribute in a vital way to God's kingdom.

Alexander Whyte was a noted preacher at St. George's Church in Edinburgh. One day a man came by to see him. On Sunday, he had invited a friend to come to church with him. Rigby, a commercial traveler, often visited Edinburgh on business. He would stay at a local hotel. He always invited some stranger to come with him to church. The man he invited on Sunday at first refused, but later at Rigby's persistence came with him. The man was so overtaken by Whyte's preaching that he came back that night and silently made a commitment of faith to Jesus Christ. Rigby shared that news with Mr. Whyte. "God bless you for telling me" Whyte said. "I thought Sunday night's sermon fell flat and I was very depressed about it." And then Whyte said: "I didn't quite catch your name," "Rigby;" the man said. "Rigby! Man," responded Whyte, "I have been looking for you for years." He ran back into his study and came back out with a huge stack of letters. He told him that he had letters from numerous men who told him about being invited to church by a man named Rigby. In his bundle of letters, twelve came from young men, four of whom had committed their lives to the ministry. All of this came about because one man invited others to church.

It may seem like a small thing, but it can be a part of our usefulness for Jesus Christ. When was the last time you invited a neighbor, a friend, or a stranger to come to church with you so that they might hear the good news of Christ? This can be a small way to be useful in his kingdom.

The Importance Of Another Opportunity

But this parable further reminds us that God gives us another chance. The gardener pleaded with the owner and said: "Wait. Let me work with this tree for another year. I will dig around it and put some manure around it. Maybe it can still produce fruit." Kenneth Bailey, professor in the Near Eastern School of Theology in Beirut, is convinced that the use of this phrase "casting on manure" is what comedians call "insult humor." Jesus had indicated that the fig tree represented the chief priests and scribes. His hearers would understand his anti-establishment use of that phrase when he declared: "I am going to spread some manure all around this tree." They knew the put-down the "mild irreverence" for the people in power. This sparkle did not hide the cutting edge of this parable.[27]

The gardener insisted: "Let's wait a while and see what will happen. Let's give the tree another chance." The scriptures tell us repeatedly that God continues to give people another opportunity to respond to his message of love. Peter denied Christ, but Jesus forgave him and gave him another chance to serve him. Peter repented and became one of the greatest spokespeople for Christ who ever lived. Mark worked with Paul for a while, but then deserted him in a foreign land. Later, he returned and worked with Paul again. The Gospel of Mark came from his pen, because he was given another chance. Paul was at first a persecutor of

---

27 Kenneth E. Bailey, *Through Peasant Eyes* (Grand Rapids: William B. Eerdmans, 1980), 84.

the Christians, but following his conversion, Christ gave him another chance, and his work changed the world. The gardener's plea reminds us of the grace of God. This parable tells us about the gospel of the second chance. No matter how great your sins are, you can come to God, find forgiveness, and an opportunity to begin again.

J. Wallace Hamilton told the story of Dr. A. J. Cronin, who was a physician for many years in England.[28] One day a young boy was brought to the hospital, desperately ill with diphtheria. A tube was inserted into his throat so he could breathe and a nurse was stationed to see that the tube remained clear. Unfortunately, she dozed off and awakened to find that the tube was blocked with membrane. Instead of cleaning the tube, she panicked and hysterically called the doctor out of sleep. When he got to the child's side, it was too late. The doctor was outraged that a child should die so needlessly and wrote out his report demanding her immediate expulsion. He called her in and read, his voice trembling with resentment, what he had written to the board of health. She stood before him in silence almost fainting with shame and remorse. "Well, have you nothing to say for yourself?" he asked. Only silence, then in a stammering plea, "Give me... give me another chance."

The doctor was shocked. She had failed at her responsibility and there was nothing else to do, as he saw it. He told her to leave, sealed his report, and retired to bed, but he was unable to sleep. A far-off word floated in and continued to whisper: "Forgive us our trespasses." The next morning, he tore up the report and gave her another chance. Later that young nurse became the head of a large hospital and one of the most honored nurses in England.

Give me another chance is our plea. We raise our voices to God and cry, "Give me another opportunity," and God forgives.

Judgment

But this parable is also about final judgment. There is a limit to God's patience. The owner in the parable says. "Yes, you work

---

28 J. Wallace Hamilton. *Horns and Halos in Human Nature* (New York: Fleming H. Revell Co., 1954), 94-95.

on the tree for a while longer. But if it does not produce at the end of this year, cut it down." There is a limit to your opportunities to respond. Jesus said, "If the salt loses its saltiness, throw it out. It is good for nothing." This is not just a scare tactic, but it is a part of the reality of life. There is a certain time for repentance, but when death comes, the time to repent is past. The opportunity to respond to the Gospel of Christ is now. The chance to repent and turn to him or else face the judgment and harsh reality of separation from God is now.

Kenneth Shamblin was a friend with a skilled doctor who was unfailing in his service to others. "I would like to know the secret of your patience. I would like to understand why it is that you have so much understanding for the burdens people carry. You never seem to quit a man because he refuses to live by his best values. Even when he is weak, you stay by him," Shamblin noted. Tears came to his eyes as he said to him, "Kenneth, I'll have to tell you how much I have been forgiven. If you knew what the grace of God had done in my own life, then you could understand why I am able to mean a little bit to so many people".[29]

Who among us; who among us; *who among us* dares not talk about how great the forgiveness of God has been in his or her life? How much more then should we be willing to acknowledge our own forgiveness, repent, and rise to serve him?

---

[29] Kenneth Shamblin, *Life Comes as Choice* (Nashville: Abingdon Press, 1967), 136.

Making Your Future

(Parables of the Tenants in the Vineyard)

Mark 12: 1-12

A giant cathedral was under construction. The foreman had rejected a large pile of stones for inclusion in the building. The architect came by later that same day and was rummaging around in the pile of stones which had been rejected and noticed a particular stone, and he quickly moved the others aside. As he examined that stone, he knew immediately that this stone was the perfect one for his purpose. He called the foreman over to him and asked, "Why have you not used this stone in the building?" "None of the others will work with it," the foreman said. "They won't fit properly." "Then you make the other stones adjust to this one," the architect said. "This is the perfect cornerstone for the cathedral." The stone which had been rejected became the chief cornerstone. This is the way Jesus ended one of his parables after he had been asked by what authority he said what he said.

The Rejected Stone

Jesus told a parable to the religious leaders and the people around him about an ancient stone that had been rejected. It was not a figure just about rocks, but about himself and his ministry. To drive home his point, he told a story about tenants in a vineyard. Eduard Schweizer, the New Testament scholar, has said that the parable about the vineyard is "the only parable in the synoptics which strongly resembles an allegory." Jesus spoke about a man who owned a vineyard. He had employed some tenants to take care of it for him, and, then, after a period of time, he sent servants to collect his money. But they thought that, since this man lived in a foreign country, they did not really need to answer to him and could get by without paying him his rent. They mistreated the servants he sent, beat them, and then, as others came, they killed some of them, and beat others. When the son of the owner was finally sent, they said: "If we kill him, then the vineyard will be ours." So, they killed him. Jesus then asked the crowd, "What would the owner do when that happened?" The answer was, of course, that he would come with harsh judgment against the tenants.

An Allegorical Interpretation

The allegorical part of this parable is this. The owner of the vineyard is God himself. The vineyard represents the children of Israel. The servants, of course, are the prophets down through the centuries who came to warn Israel about the judgment of God and they called them to repentance. The people beat some and killed others. Finally, God sent his son, Jesus Christ himself, thinking that surely, they would respond to him, but they crucified him. Jesus knew that his death was coming, but he told them that the very one they thought they had defeated would become the chief cornerstone on which God's kingdom will be built.

The Parable Speaks To Us

What does this story have to do with us today? First, let us consider what this parable has to say about us as men and women. The vineyard, of course, as is described in this parable, received many advantages, and favors from the owner. The nation Israel itself had been a very favored people — God's chosen people. They had received the great blessings, benefits, and generosity of God. So have you, and so have I. We are, indeed, a very favored people. We have seen that God down through the centuries has been not only a very generous God but that he has been a very patient God toward us. We, too, know something of having received favor from God.

The Importance Of Freedom

But notice also that with God's great generosity goes the requirement of freedom. He gave the tenants the opportunity to use the vineyard as they would. They were responsible to care for it, and they had the freedom to manage it as they would. God has also given to you and to me freedom to learn to live in his world. Often, we misuse this freedom, thinking that it gives us total liberty to do anything we want with it. God has never given any of us total freedom. It is always responsible freedom.

You have seen sometimes what has happened when a school teacher goes out of the room. The kids go absolutely wild. Somebody may run over and put his feet up on the teacher's desk. Some begin to throw paper balls back and forth across the room. Another goes to the blackboard and starts writing on it. Others may turn desks over. That, of course, is not the kind of freedom that is expected in school rooms, whether the teacher is present in the room or not. That is freedom abused; freedom gone wild.

In this vineyard, they had freedom. They presumed that because they were there, they had squatters' right and could do with the vineyard as they chose, no matter what the owner wanted. Often this is true with you and me. We think we have the freedom which God has given to us to do as we please in life, without regard for God or even sometimes for others. With freedom, there must always be some sense of direction and proper use of that freedom.

Many have thought that *Alice In Wonderland* was simply a children's book. But there are more adult insights in that book than you and I often can imagine. Alice encountered the Cheshire cat in her path, and she asked; "Would you tell me, please, which way I ought to go from here?" The cat replied, "That depends a great deal on where you want to go." "Oh, I don't care much." "Then it really doesn't matter much which way you go." "But," Alice responded in a rather defiant way, "I want to go somewhere." "Oh," the cat said, "You are sure to do that."

Whenever we use our freedom, we can be sure we will go somewhere. We are free to take whatever direction we may want. But that freedom may sometimes merely be motion without movement, or it may be only talking without thinking. Sometimes we are busy going without goals or moving without finding meaning in what we do. But, yes, we shall go somewhere when we exercise our freedom.

J. Wallace Hamilton shared a story that his father, who was a farmer, used to love to tell about a man who wanted to buy a saddle horse for his family. The farmer told the city lawyer that he could have the horse, "if he could ketch 'em." The lawyer and his two sons went to the pasture to get him, and after about three hours, they came back with the animal. The farmer said to the city attorney, "There are two things I have to tell you about this horse before I take your money. In the first place, he's awful hard to ketch." The man knew that already since he had spent three hours trying to catch the horse. "The second thing," the farmer said with a wink, "he's not worth a durn when you've ketched him."[30]

There are some folks in life who are so busy chasing after things which they think they have the freedom to do, yet when they get them, they discover that they are really not worth having. Some spend their whole lives pursuing material goals and when they get them, they realize that they do not satisfy them. We have the freedom to lie, but when we lie, we lose integrity. We have the freedom to cheat, but when we cheat, we lose the educational value of learning. We have the freedom not to worship God, but when we don't worship, we lose the power of God's presence. We have the freedom to deny God, but when we do, we lose the power of his fellowship. We have the freedom to misuse others, but when we do, we do not practice justice. We can have the freedom to hate, but we lose love. We have the freedom to love or to hate. We have the freedom to do right and not wrong. We have the freedom to be courageous and not cowardly. We have the freedom to do good and not evil. God gives us freedom. We must choose how we shall use it. We can do evil with it or we can do good. Sometimes those things which we are pursuing with all our efforts become only illusions in our hands or puffs of smoke that have no purpose or meaning.

There is no real freedom without the responsibility that is connected and embedded with it. When my children began to

---

30 J. Wallace Hamilton, *Where Now Is Thy God?* (Old Tappan, New Jersey: Fleming H. Revell Co., 1969), 108.

drive and they wanted to use the car, one of the messages that I, like all parents, told them was, "Oh yes, you have the freedom to drive, but with it must go responsible driving, and responsible habits in the use of a car." No real freedom comes in life without the added cost of responsibility connected with it.

God's Judgment

Second, note what this parable tells us about God. We live with freedom but with this freedom we are assured that we always live under God's judgment. Even as patient and good as God is, there is always his discerning judgment, because sin cannot stand in the sight of God without being judged. We cannot continuously abuse God's prophets, continuously abuse God's ways, and not expect to avoid the judgment of God. The scriptures are clear on this issue. Some people say, "I can do anything I want to," and they focus their life totally upon themselves. Life is self-centered, self-directed; what can the world do for me. Some people are like the farmer who said, "I am not greedy. I just want all the land that adjoins mine." Some of us want everything in life that touches us to be ours. We are like the young man who said, "I let all the stops out to do anything I wanted to do and then life crashed in." Judgment always comes with the misuse of freedom. God is patient and loving, but he desires that we learn to live a righteous life and a life in fellowship with him.

A Call To Repentance

In this parable, Jesus is speaking not simply about the judgment of God, but he tells us about God's call to come again into his power and presence. It is a call to repentance. It is a call which reminds us that we do not have to continue in waywardness. We do not have to continue moving away from God, but it is a call to come back and walk in communion with him. It is a reminder of God's continuous opportunity for us to receive his love.

If you drive down Interstate 40 between Knoxville, Tennessee and Asheville, North Carolina, you find it is a rather mountainous section of the country where the highway winds its way through the beautiful hills. As one drives down some of the very steep hills, you can see a "run-away" ramp or an "escape road" which is located at the end of a long descent in case your truck or your car has its brakes fail. It gives the driver someplace to go rather than over the edge. This side ramp leads uphill so you can stop and not go over the mountainside to your destruction. As I have driven down the mountain, fortunately, I have never had to use one of those roads. But I have seen trucks come down those hills almost flying sometimes, and I have wondered what in the world would happen if their brakes failed. One time I rounded one of the curves as I slowly moved down the hillside, and the sign at the entrance to one of those escape roads read "Run Away Ramp closed." It would be a great tragedy to have your brakes fail and then discover that the "escape road" or "run-away" ramp was closed.

The good news of the gospel is this. God has provided for us an avenue back to him. Life does not have to end at dead-end streets. It doesn't have to end in chaos and confusion. We discover an avenue which moves us into the grace and arms of a God who loves us and cares for us. God is always reaching out toward us to let us know of his love and grace. We can begin anew. There is another road which we can take. Whatever road we may have taken in life, we know we can make a "u-turn." The word repentance means "turn around." You can begin again with God. That is great good news wherever we are; we know we can start anew.

Seemingly Deaf To God

Life for some of us often becomes so daily and so routine. We become so involved in our daily work, schoolwork, our work at home, and all of our activities, that somehow or another we almost forget God in the midst of all we do. We do not seem to hear God's voice speaking to us and we do not seek to find his guidance. We listen only to our wants, needs, and desires.

I read about an annual convention of another denomination which met a number of years ago. A rather hard of hearing preacher was sitting down close to the front near the speaker's platform. He kept nudging a fellow pastor and asking: "What did he say? What did he say?" The minister on the platform could even hear him. Finally, his friend said, "Keep quiet. I told you I'd tell you if he ever says anything." Now that is a frustrating experience if you are a speaker.

Too many of us, however, have become deaf to God in our daily life and cannot hear God's voice addressing us. But hear this! God has said something that we need to hear in the midst of our routines, and "dailyness" of life and it concerns the good news which God has for us. We can begin again. Though we are sinners, God's grace has come into the world to show us God's powerful love. his son has come to give us new life — a new beginning. This leads us to the next point.

The Sacrificial Love Of God

Third, this parable is a great declaration about the sacrificial love of God. Though the tenants, who represent the rulers of Israel; though the people of Israel, though you and I as a part of the church of God, may reject God and may turn against God, the great good news is that God continues to love us. He comes to us with a message of hope and forgiveness and the opportunity to begin anew. This parable proclaims the eternal goodness of God. It proclaims the eternal love of God. God did not suddenly become loving in Jesus Christ. God has always been a loving God. He sent his love through prophets down through the centuries who told people of God's grace, and even then, they turned away from it. God finally sent his love in Jesus Christ to show us supremely how much he cared for us. The very stone which the builders had rejected became the chief cornerstone.

In the ancient times, when Psalm 118 was used in worship, it was a processional hymn. The people, led by the king, would approach the gates of the temple, and begin to sing: "Lift up the gates." Then the temple priest would raise the gates, and the people would march through the gates with the king leading them, and they would cry: "The stone which the builders have rejected has become the chief cornerstone." For them, of course, the rejected stone was Israel. The nation, which had seemed so small and insignificant, had been chosen by God to be a great nation in the world through which God would declare his grace. Today the New Testament church declares that this stone is Jesus Christ. God has revealed himself through Christ, and Christ has become the chief cornerstone. Through Christ we experience the grace, love, and power of the God who redeems us and draws us back to himself.

The Unlikely Chosen

One of the interesting features of this parable, seen both in the metaphor from the Old Testament and in the parable of Jesus, is the assertion that God often turns the values of humankind on their head. Sometimes we think that the "great" people are those who have power and influence. But God's standard reveals that the stone which was rejected became the chief cornerstone. The nation which was rejected became God's powerful nation to declare his message of grace. The one crucified became the one who was able to save others. The very least now becomes the most important. The unlikely becomes the possible. The last becomes the first. The humiliated becomes the honored. With God, there is often a great reversal. God reaches back and changes and twists human values to show us that his value is on a different level often than the world's standards. He chooses sometimes to work through the helpless and the rejected to bring about good news, mercy, and love. Most of that he does through us and other unlikely vessels.

Hans Sach has a book titled *Masks of Love and Life*. There is a chapter in this book with a fascinating title, "Locked in Rooms with Open Doors." Reflect on that for a while. How many of us remain locked in rooms with open doors, but we do not open them and go through them. We are locked in rooms of old grudges, old sins, old habits, old ways, and we cannot find forgiveness, love, and grace even when the door is open all the time. We are locked in old traditions, old ways, and old thoughts. We are locked in all kinds of practices and patterns when all the time the door is open. Because God has opened it for us, we can walk through it and find forgiveness and newness of life to begin again. That is great, marvelous good news for all of us, and we need to hear it.

We, too, have freedom to choose what path we will take. Will it be the path of selfishness? Will you use your freedom to turn to God or away from God? God gives you freedom to choose. God will not force you to respond to his love. God will continually seek to reach you with his love. He will not give up. You are given the freedom to say yes or no, to respond or reject that love. The choice is yours. Don't remain locked in. Choose.

We are not locked in, but the doors are open and we can reach up to become more of what God wants us to be. The power and presence of God draws us by his sacrificial love to be more than we can ever imagine. Don't run away. Don't use your freedom to move away from God. Use your freedom to draw upon the power of his grace, and you will be amazed at how marvelous his grace enables you to experience authentic life.

A Triumphant Note Of Joy

(Parables of the Lost Sheep and the Lost Coin)

Luke 15:3-10

The scribes and Pharisees were quite upset with Jesus. He was eating with sinners — not just talking with them — but actually eating with them. Table traditions in the ancient world were taken very seriously. A rich man might share his food with someone in need to show his generosity, but he would never eat with them. To eat with someone was a sign of trust, brotherhood, and peace. Because he associated with sinners, Jesus received criticism, taunts, and sneers, from the scribes and Pharisees.

Before you quickly condemn the scribes and Pharisees, you might place their concern in a contemporary setting. Picture Jesus, rather than coming to our church and associating with us, going to the worst part of our city — to the red-light district — entering a local tavern, and sitting down and eating with streetwalkers and notorious criminals. Most of you, who consider yourself respectable, would not be too thrilled with that kind of behavior from your minister. You expect him to associate with the "right" kind of people. The Pharisees did not like the company Jesus was keeping. It is interesting to observe that three of the most beautiful parables of Jesus — the lost sheep, the lost coin, and the lost son were told in response to taunts from the scribes and Pharisees. These stories were Jesus' response to sneers that were directed at him because of the company he kept.

The Lost Sheep

Notice first the parable about the lost sheep. Before you begin to think that this story is simply a "sweet" parable about sheep, you must bear in mind that the shepherd was not seen as such an honorable profession by the Pharisees in the day of Jesus. In fact, shepherds were linked with the sinners — the outcasts of society. It is a strange irony that the same people, who could show reverence for the ancient shepherd like Moses, or even describe God as a shepherd in their Old Testament writings, would look with disdain on shepherds of their own day. Shepherds were linked with peddlers, excise-men, tanners, donkey drivers, and tax collectors as people who followed dishonorable occupations. Their work made them "unclean." When Jesus began his parable by asking his listeners to suppose that they were a shepherd, he was directing this at the scribes and Pharisees. This suggestion would have shocked them, but Jesus offered it probably with a twinkle in his eye and humor in his voice. The crowd may have nudged each other and said: "Look, look what he is saying about them."

Lost

His listeners were familiar with the shepherd image. "Suppose there is a shepherd who has a hundred sheep," Jesus said, "and he has one that is lost." It is interesting to note that Jesus seldom used the word "sinners" to describe those who were immoral or drifting in life. He almost always used the word "lost," and he used it with tenderness and compassion. It was not used in ridicule or disdain or to heap anger or hostility upon them. His word "lost" reminded them of the compassion of God.

Jesus said that some people are lost, just like a sheep. A sheep wanders off seeking to find better grass. It begins to wander and drift aimlessly, moving without direction, simply following the easiest path before it. George Buttrick once wrote about a farmer who found a stray. "How do they get lost?" a city man asked. "They just nibble themselves lost," said the farmer. "They keep their heads down, wander from one green tuft to another, come to a hole in the fence — and never can find a hole by which to get back again"[31] That is a contemporary image of sheep raising because in the ancient world, there were no fences. But like a sheep, many of us, without any thought of being immoral, are

31 George Buttrick, editor, *The Interpreter's Bible*, vol. VIII (New York: Abingdon Press, 1952), 265.

drifting aimlessly without a polestar, a fixed direction, or a compass. There is no goal or anchor. We are busy going. Many have wandered away into the wilderness of life without direction, meaning or purpose. There is no thought of rebellion or turning against somebody or something. They are caught in the stream of life and seem to be enjoying whatever they are doing until they suddenly realize that they don't know where they are. They are lost. They have joined the wanderers of life. They are drifting like plankton in the sea, carried by the currents with no control over their direction. These people do not intend to do any harm or get in trouble. They do not want to rebel, but, like a sheep, they just follow the easiest path without forethought or planning. They follow the easiest way without considering the consequences for themselves, family, or others.

The word "lost" sounds like a distant bell echoing through these parables, calling people to come home again. Lost. Some are lost in their burden of busy bureaucracy. Others are lost in their rat race of routine running. Others are lost in daily decisions or carried away by pleasant pleasure. Some are picked to pieces by perplexity. Others are lost in the glittering garden of gadgets. Some are lost in the tempting taste for things while others are lost in secret sins and sorrows, lonely laments, or family frustrations. Lost - lost are these modern-day Adam and Eve — somewhere on the other side of nowhere — east of Eden. They are searching, groping to find some place, direction, hope, or meaning. But lost. These parables do not address people centuries ago, but they have a message for us today.

Lostness

This parable speaks not only about lostness but "lostness". Each of these parables speaks about a loss. There was a loss to the shepherd, to the woman who lost her coin, and a father who lost a son — the prodigal son. The shepherd goes after his property — the sheep; a woman searches for her coin. God has lost something that is his. We were created in his image. He is anxious about us. Here we see the concern of God. He comes after us. Do you not sense that God misses you, loves you, longs for you, wants to find you, and wants to bring you home again? Do you not sense in your lostness that there is a loss to God? He is seeking to call you home again.

Searches

Notice that the shepherd went searching for the lost sheep. That doesn't mean that he abandoned the ninety and nine and left them on their own. He either put them safely in a sheepfold, maybe a cave, where no wild animals could harm them. But most likely, there was another shepherd who could watch these sheep while he went searching for the one that was lost. He would never risk the lives of the others just for the sake of the one. Someone guarded the ninety and nine while he looked for the one.

Searches Until Finds

The image is that the shepherd searches "until." This parable reveals the nature of God. He is like a shepherd or a woman who search until they find. In many religions, men and women search for God, but in Christianity, God searches for us. He doesn't say: "Oh, they'll come back." He goes after them himself. This is the gospel within the gospel. These parables depict the heart of the New Testament images about God. God is not remote, distant, uncaring, or unfeeling. He is a God who comes searching after us in our lostness to bring us back into fellowship with him. The New Testament image of God is stated in Paul's words: "Though he was rich, yet for your sake became poor" (2 Corinthians 8:9). This is a picture of the God who so loves us that he gave his only son to draw us back to himself. It is the secret of the incarnation. Here is the explanation for the costly sacrifice of God. He wants to bring us back from our wandering, our lostness, into his presence. He searches for the lost sheep and the lost coin "until" he finds.

The Importance Of All

The search reveals their worth. This parable reminds us of how valuable we are to God. Sometimes a person feels that he or she does not count or is not important. Remember you will never be at a place in your life, even at its lowest point, where God does not still see you as a person of worth. Even, if you are in the gutter of despair, or on the backside of the wilderness of sin, God still sees you as a person of worth, and he will come searching for you to bring you home again. God loves you; he cares for you. Jesus has reminded us that God knows the very hairs of our head, and that a sparrow does not fall to the ground without his knowledge. If God is aware of these small things, how much more aware is he of us? The parables of the lost sheep and lost coin indicate the worth God feels for us.

Several years ago, when the space shuttle exploded on takeoff, the horror of that disaster greatly shocked our country. Our concern was not primarily with the loss of a space shuttle, though it cost more than a billion dollars, but with the people who were killed. If you and I are concerned about people, how much more is God concerned about them? He goes searching after us to bring us home again to him. When the shepherd finds the sheep, he doesn't say to the sheep: "Oh, you awful animal, why have you done this?" He doesn't condemn it, chastise it, whip it, or punish it. He gently brings the animal back.

A Cast Down Position

Sometimes a sheep may be found in what is called a "cast down" position. A sheep may wander off from the rest of the flock. It may get buried too deeply in the ground, or too deeply in the grass; then it becomes trapped. It may turn over on its back. While the sheep is on its back, a gas begins to develop inside the animal. No matter how hard it struggles, the sheep cannot get right side up again. The more it struggles, the worse it gets. Unless the shepherd finds the sheep, it will become easy prey for the buzzards and wild animals. When the shepherd finds the sheep in this kind of condition, he gently strokes the animal, slowly turns it over, and then places the sheep on his shoulders and brings it back to the flock again.

We don't know if the animal was caught in a crevice or a thicket. We don't know if the animal was cast down. When the shepherd finds the sheep, maybe it is still nibbling at the grass, not even aware that it has drifted away from the others. We don't know. The shepherd finds him and brings him home again.

Restoration

Not only did he find the lost sheep, but he restored it to the flock. There is joy for the shepherd in finding the lost sheep. But there is joy not only by the shepherd, but by the whole community as he returns home at night and says, "Look, I have found the lost sheep." There are some scholars who questioned whether shepherds brought their flocks back home at night. But studies have shown that poor herdsmen would drive their flocks back to their small villages. There both partners and family would rejoice with the shepherd in the finding of the sheep.

Who are the ninety and nine that Jesus said didn't need to repent? They were certainly not the scribes and Pharisees. because Jesus constantly spoke about their corruption. Again, and again, he directed harsh words to these religious people. The reference to the ninety and nine who didn't need repentance is likely the angels. They are already in the presence of God and do not need to repent.

The Good Shepherd

Jesus often drew upon the image of the shepherd. "All like sheep have gone astray," and need a shepherd. Jesus is the "Good Shepherd." "I am the Good Shepherd; I know my sheep and they hear my voice and they follow me." Even today, if shepherds mix their flocks of sheep in a sheepfold overnight, the next morning each shepherd can call to his sheep and they will recognize his voice and follow him. Jesus says, "I know my sheep and my sheep know my voice and they follow me." Jesus is the Good Shepherd. He has revealed the God who comes seeking us to bring us back from our wandering to him.

The Lost Coin

Look for a moment at the parable of the lost coin. You might ask the question, "Why should anyone be concerned with the loss of a coin that is worth only about twenty cents in today's money?" But in that day, its value was the equivalent of a day's wage. She may have lost the money she was going to use to pay the temple tax. That coin would have been enough to pay her taxes for the whole year. The lost coin may have been a part of her heirloom or dowry. Certain coins were given to a woman by her father and they could not be taken away from her no matter what happened. Coins of this kind were often worn at the end of her braids or on her veil. Most likely, however, these coins were a part of her headdress made up of ten silver pieces which were a sign of a married woman. Our wedding ring today would be the closest equivalent. She or her husband may have worked for years to have enough money to put these ten coins there. They were often strung together as a frontlet around her forehead. In some way or another she had lost one of these coins in her house. She searched diligently for it.

It was much harder to find something if it were lost then than it would be in our house today. To understand the problem, you have to know a little about what houses were like in biblical times. Most of them were simple structures made of sticks and mud. The houses of poor people often had no windows at all — only a door. The floors were dirt and covered with dried rushes and reeds. If she lost one of her coins, it was like looking for a needle in a haystack. She had a palm branch broom which she used to sweep through the dried plants to see if she could dislodge the coin. An oil lamp was lit to furnish some light for the search. She had lost something of great worth to her, and did everything she could to find it.

Out Of Circulation

Some of us are lost like coins, are we not? We are out of circulation. The value of one's life, like the value of the coin, is still there, but unless your life is in circulation, you may feel it has no purpose. There are some who feel useless and cut off from life. They do not feel that they are contributing anything worthwhile. They are lost to helpful causes. They have no real direction or sense of usefulness. But if these people are "found" again, they can still have possibilities for a meaningful and purposeful life.

Not Our Fault

Sometimes, like the coin, your lostness is not your own fault. In many ways, we are the recipients of what somebody else has done.

We don't like to admit this, but it is true. There are some things that happen to people in life over which they have absolutely no control or responsibility. For example, there is a young baby born blind because his mother had syphilis. Who did sin? This child or the parents? The child comes into the world blind, because of the sinfulness of the parents. Here is another child who is reared in a home where it is taught from the time that it can walk that cheating and stealing are acceptable. Who is primarily at fault when later the child is arrested for stealing? The parents or the child? Many children are the victims of circumstances. To get free from them, they should be educated and shown a different way. It will not be easy to free them from their surroundings and influence. This is not to exclude all personal responsibility for a person's actions. But it is to affirm that everything that happens to a person is not necessarily his or her fault alone. There are some who are caught in a long line of poverty which goes back for generations, and it will take much training and help to liberate them from their past. They are out of circulation and desperately need help.

God's Disturbance

The woman searched diligently for the coin. To do this, she had to disturb the dried reeds and rushes on the floor. Sometimes when God comes into our life to bring us his redemption, he must disturb us. He must challenge our prejudices, bigotry, desires, and attitude. He will challenge us and disturb us, if necessary, so his salvation can come into our life. Sometimes he turns our life upside down. We may not like it, but God sets his own agenda for our lives. God will not leave us undisturbed or unchallenged. When the women found the coin, she rejoiced and called her friends together and asked them to celebrate with her.

These parables remind you and me today, as we gather in our home or church, that we can always have hope. Thank goodness God does not treat us as we deserve. When the sheep chose to go its way, it didn't think about the shepherd's concern. The sheep had chosen its own way. But the shepherd went after it anyway. The coin could not do anything to help in finding itself. The woman thought it was valuable and began searching for it.

God doesn't see any of us as hopeless or useless. He sees us as people of worth, and he comes after us to love us, redeem us, and bring us back home to him. Jesus looked into the face of Simon and he saw the possibility of one who could become Peter. He looked into the face of doubting Thomas and saw the possibility of one who could be a strong believer. He looked into the face of the sinner Mary Magdalene and saw the possibility of a restored saint. He looked at Saul the militant persecutor of the church and saw the possibility of a great missionary. God looks into your life and my life and sees the possibilities of what we can be by his grace. No one is seen as hopeless.

The Note Of Joy

These parables focus on a triumphant note of joy. There is great joy in heaven, Jesus says, when a sinner repents. The God who created us restores us to fellowship again. One of the great Jewish scholars, Claude Montefiore, has noted that the image of God as a seeking God is a completely new image in Judaism. "Here is a new figure which has never ceased to play its great part in the moral and religious development of the world."[32]

If I were an artist, I would try to paint two pictures of these parables. In one I would show an old mud hut with no windows and an open door. Inside, a woman could be seen down on her knees buried partially in the dried rushes and reeds. A palm branch broom would be lying beside her. An oil lamp would be nearby to give her some light. A bright coin would be glistening in the sunlight as she held it in her hand, and a happy smile would be on her face, because she had found her lost coin.

If I were painting a picture of the parable of the lost sheep, I would want it to be a large painting. Down in the lower portion of the picture, I would have the ninety and nine sheep in a sheepfold safely guarded by another shepherd. There would be a small stream where the sheep could get water and green grass. Rocks piled high with thistles on top of the rocks would surround the sheepfold. Rugged terrain would stretch up the mountainside

---

32 Claude Montefiore, *The Synoptic Gospels*, vol. II (London: Macmillan and Co., 1909), 520.

away from the sheepfold. There would be spots of grass along the way, but briars, thistles, and boulders would dominate the landscape. Far up the mountain, you could see some wild animals, and a buzzard or two in the trees. Then the central figure would emerge. A shepherd, rugged in his appearance, would be visible walking down the mountain through the brush with the sheep draped tenderly across his shoulders as he brought the lost sheep home.

Like the shepherd, God comes looking for us. Some of you have wandered away from God, and he is calling you to come home. He is seeking you and wants to find you. Turn to him and sense his love. Some of you do not feel at home anymore. You don't feel at home in your house, at work, or anywhere. God is seeking to call you back to him so you can find togetherness again. God is seeking to give you joy. The greatest joy which any person can experience is the joy that comes in knowing Jesus Christ as the Good Shepherd. "I've come that you might have life and have it more abundantly." Jesus said. "I've come that your joy might be made full." He is searching for you. I hope that you will let him find you and experience a triumphant note of joy.

When you and I have found this inner joy, then we should become what Archbishop Tutu describes as "a reservoir of joy, an oasis of peace, a pool of serenity that can ripple out to all those around you."[33] Through this joy we have found in Christ, we then reach out to others in love, compassion, and generosity. We feel we must share what we have experienced.

---

33 Delai Lama and Desmond Tutu (with Douglas Abrams) *The Book of Joy* (New York: Avery: An Imprint of Penguin Random House, 2016), 63.

Building For The Long Haul

(Parable of the Rock Foundation)

Luke 6: 46-49

William Golden has a novel titled *The Spire*. The setting is in the Bavarian Alps. The story focuses on an elderly priest who had been the pastor of an old, dilapidated church for a long time. His dream was to put a 450-foot spire on top of the church building to remind the farmers and herdsmen of God while they worked. But it was a poor congregation, and the church building was also poorly constructed. Architects and engineers told him not to put a spire on top of the building. They said that it simply could not support that kind of load.

When the priest was eighty years old, the only wealthy member of the congregation died and left all her resources to the church. At last, he saw his opportunity to build his 450-foot spire. And the work soon began. In spite of people like the engineers and others who said, "Don't do it," the old priest insisted they begin the construction. In erecting the 450-foot spire, the spiritual life of the church was destroyed. Daily mass could not be held because of all the construction noise and the profanity of the workers on the scaffolds. Most of the workers quit because the construction was too dangerous. The priest had to spend many hours trying to get others to join his work crew until the spire was finished. After the spire was finally finished, it was not the permanent witness which the priest had hoped it would be. Every time the wind blew, the spire creaked, groaned, and moved as though it would topple over. He erected his spire, but he had destroyed his church in the process. The foundation of the church was simply not strong enough to sustain it.

A Parable From A Carpenter

Jesus knew a whole lot about building houses. After all he was a carpenter. He obviously had built many things as a carpenter, houses included. One of the parables he told his disciples was about constructing houses and the necessity of having a firm foundation for a house. Both the gospels of Matthew and Luke record the parable of building a house on a strong foundation. There are slightly different versions of this parable in the two accounts. In Matthew's Gospel, the house was probably built in a creek bed or right by it on sandy soil. You might ask, "Why would somebody build in such a place?" Well, in the first place, it was easy. You could erect the house quickly and simply there. It didn't rain much in Palestine. This location was close to water. It also protected them from the wind that might be blowing. Once in a generation, however, the snows would melt on the mountains nearby, and the water would come rushing down through the empty riverbed. The houses that had been built in the creek bed or beside it would be destroyed. It likely seems foolish to us today for people to build in places like that. But you must remember that Palestine didn't have large bodies of water. The word bridge does not even occur in the New Testament.

Luke's version of this story focuses on the necessity of getting down to the rock foundation on which one needs to build a secure house. Dig down until you can find a rock foundation that will sustain a house, so that when the storms come, the house will not collapse. The truth is basically the same in each parable. It is necessary to secure a firm foundation for one's house or else the storms will destroy it.

Jesus Is The Foundation

This parable comes at the end of the Sermon on the Mount in the Gospel of Matthew. In Luke's version, it is placed at the end of the Sermon on the Plain. Jesus had presented his chief teachings, and then he told a parable to illustrate the truth of his message. Let us examine this familiar parable and its message for us today. One of the lessons I think that Jesus is teaching us in this parable is that he himself — his life, example, and teachings

— is the foundation on which his church is built. Paul will write later to the Corinthians, "For no other foundation can anyone lay than that which is laid, which is Jesus Christ" (1 Corinthians. 3:11). Jesus described himself as the chief cornerstone. He and his teachings are the foundation which undergirds the church. Some want Jesus to remain a teacher and mainly a teacher who taught two thousand years ago. They recognize him as a teacher who gave us some great lessons and high moral principles for life. But they want to keep Jesus confined to the past. If Jesus is back there someplace in the past, then he doesn't affect us here in the present.

A Call To Discipleship

In this parable and in many other places in the New Testament, Jesus reminds his listeners of his ultimate authority. Jesus placed himself at the center of his teachings. Remember that Jesus called people into discipleship. He wanted people first of all to commit their lives to him and his teachings.

A fascinating story that arises out of wartime recounts an experience of the brilliant Naval Commander Admiral Nelson, who had captured one of the ships which had engaged him in battle. Admiral Nelson was noted as being a gentleman. When he boarded the ship, the defeated captain extended his hand to shake hands with the naval commander. But Admiral Nelson said to him: "First your sword, then your hand."

Jesus Christ calls us into discipleship first. Before we can really follow his teachings, we must commit our lives to him. This call is a call to surrender. This means that you cannot keep some secret corner of your life from Christ. You cannot have some attic room cluttered with old memories and sins that you want to cling to and still follow Christ. You cannot keep some dark basement level of your life filled with all kinds of remorse and sins and continue to commit your life to Christ. He calls you first to surrender your life to him and experience the transforming power of God's grace. Christ is the foundation upon which life is built, and his teachings provide directions and insight into life1s deepest meaning. We have to open our lives completely to him.

A Call To Action

Secondly, this parable teaches us that religion is to be lived out in life. Jesus states that religion, when it is real religion, must take the form of action. "Listen."

Jesus said. Hearing is not enough. We must "do." We are not called simply to admire the teachings of Jesus, nor just agree with them. He calls us to let his teachings permeate our very being; take on flesh; be reincarnated in our living each and every day.

Halford Luccock told a story about an experience that took place in deep Africa years ago, when some missionaries sent a plow to the natives. The Africans had never seen a plow before. They didn't know what it was or what to do with it. They assumed that it was some kind of god and put the plow on a pedestal and worshiped it. The plow did not reach down into the soil and cut through the ground so that it could be used for planting crops. To limit the plow to admiration is to make it useless. The teachings of Jesus were not meant to be put on some pedestal and admired. They are to be lived out in our daily life.

Others like to talk about how wonderful they think the teachings of Jesus are. Many church groups spend a great deal of time talking about the teachings of Jesus. We study them, discuss them, debate them, pray about them, and sometimes argue about them. But that is not enough. It is insufficient merely to talk or to teach the lessons from Jesus. We must live them. If his teachings are to be a meaningful part of our life, they have to permeate our whole being. His teachings are to be lived out in our home, business, and leisure. Jesus has called us to do his word. Hearing and talking about his teachings are not sufficient.

The church relates clearly that redemption is by the grace of God. We are thankful that we are redeemed by God's love. But in the next breath, God has called us to live out our lives of faith. The epistle of James reminds us that "faith without works is dead" (James 2:26). If you talk about having religion and then you don't live it in your life, that claim is simply a lie. Faith without works is dead. Jesus says, "You will know my disciples by their fruits." His disciples will be known by whether or not they live out what they say about him.

You may have seen the cartoon a number of years ago. A father is standing over a barbecue pit, roasting a hug piece of meat over hot coals. He turns to his son and says: "Now son, this is the third fatted calf we have roasted for you. When are you going to settle down?" There are some folks who think forgiveness is a wonderful word. They want to hear it. They may sometimes approach their pastor or another counselor and tell him about some secret sin in their life and ask for God's forgiveness. They then go back and keep on committing the same sin. They feel forgiven, but real repentance means to stop doing what you have been doing! Change your life! You can't cling to the same old sins in your life and talk about the power of God's forgiving grace being real to you. A person who has genuinely experienced forgiveness will give up a sinful way of life and turn to a new way of living.

A woman came to see her pastor one day. She told him that she felt that she needed to share with him her sin of self-centeredness and selfishness. She wanted to experience the forgiveness of God's grace and overcome her self-centeredness. The pastor listened to her confession and then prayed with her. When they finished, she got up and said: "Oh, I feel so much better." "Wait!" her pastor said. "We haven't finished. I want you to go each week to the children's hospital and spend two hours every week helping those children. You will get out of your own self-centeredness when you do something for others. This will give life to your confession and make your forgiveness real." A life that has felt the power of the teachings of Christ will be a life that follows daily his teachings.

Construction Continues Every Day

Thirdly, we are conscious that we are building the house of our life every day. From the time we were born, the foundation of our life is being laid. Parents, teachers, friends, and people we meet in life — all have an impact on the foundation and structure of our lives. A house is not complete if all the bricks, lumber, beams, or mortar are merely lying on the ground in piles or stacked up. The elements that go into the structure are built into it day by day, sometimes hour by hour, and year by year. During all of this time, the house of your life — your character — is being built. The foundation is laid. The walls are raised and then the beams, insulation, electricity, plumbing, siding, bricks, the roof, and everything else slowly becomes a part of the structure. Ever so slowly, your life is being built. Your soul is dyed the color of your thoughts and the impact of your friends, where you go, what you do, and what others say to you. You are gradually being built and rebuilt all the time. A young girl turned to her mother as an elderly lady left their home after a brief visit. "Mother," the daughter said. "You know I really wouldn't mind growing old if I could be like Mrs. Smith. She is lovely, sweet, serene, and lovable." "I know what you mean," her mother said. "But honey, she doesn't impress me as a piece of work that was made in a hurry. You had better begin working on your life now." And we are. Every moment, every hour, you are in process of making who you are and what you will become.

Must Live In The House You Make

But fourthly, remember you have to live in the house you make. You have to live in whatever kind of structure you make of your life. One of the expressions I frequently hear from a number of people is "If only I!" "If only I had done this." Or, "If only I had not done that." "If only I hadn't married John." "If only I had married Janet." We often live a life of regrets, because we don't always like what we have made of our lives. Whether you make a solid foundation for your life or lay an inadequate base, filled with flaws, you have got to live in what you construct. You determine every day whether you are building your life on a solid rock foundation that will sustain you when difficulties come or whether you are building on sand in a riverbed.

One of my favorite theologians is Charles Schulz. In one of the comic strips which I clipped from the Sunday paper years ago, Linus is building sandcastles on the beach. You have never seen such beautiful sandcastles. They seem to cover yards and yards on the beach. He has built huge towers and structures, rich with vivid details. Then the rains began to fall on his sandcastles.

They slowly dissolve under the impact of the storm. Linus speaks only in the last frame. "There is a lesson here somewhere," he observes, "but I am not sure what it is."

But you astute biblical scholars are, aren't you? You know that Charles Schulz has reached right into the Scriptures to this parable and has put a lesson about life on the comic page. You can't build your life on sandcastles and expect them to endure in the storms. I know you have seen pictures in the newspaper from some sections in Kentucky where whole houses have disappeared, because they were built over a cavern. Nobody in his right mind is going to build a house over a cavern if he or she knows it. But sometimes the builder didn't know it. When the storms came, the ground slowly began to disintegrate and the house fell into the hole in the ground. When we lived in Louisiana, we observed that some houses did not have the foundational base and had to be built on pilings. I know one couple in our church in Louisiana that did not build their house on pilings and later had to spend more to put pilings under their house than the house had cost them originally. Without a solid foundation, a house — a life — collapses. Jesus tells us to build our life on principles and teachings that can undergird and sustain us in the tough times that will come.

Storms Are Certain

Be assured fifthly that storms will come. We can't avoid all the storms in life. There is no promise in the scriptures that being a Christian means we are exempt from the storm. Storms of all kinds will come. Sometimes these storms will be sickness, grief, rejection, criticism, loss of a job, problems with children or parents. Who knows? Storms of all kinds come into our lives.

What do we do when the storms come? The reaction of some of us is to take the first bus or plane that comes along and get away from our problems. We want to flee. Some people flee into drugs or alcohol. Others flee into pleasure pursuits. Unable to face our difficulties, we try to run. But running away from the storms doesn't remove them. We discover that we sometimes encounter even more difficult storms down the escape avenues which we have taken. Storms will come, and we have to learn to reach back and find those supports which have been built in calm weather to enable us to face the storms.

Dr. George Buttrick, who was pastor for many years in New York City, told about a church member who came into his study and recounted a horrid experience that he had just had. He had been picked up near his office by some gangsters and driven to the edge of town. They warned him that if he did not leave town or refuse to testify in a case, they were going to kill him. Dr. Buttrick said, "What did you do?" "I prayed," the man said. "Then I told them that I had to share what I knew. Whatever you are going to do to me, do quickly." He said that for some strange reason, the gangsters just stood there for a moment and looked at him, then they put him in their car and drove him back to the city and let him out near the church. I had to tell somebody, so I just came to tell you." "Why do you think, when you came to such a test as this, you were able to be true to the highest within you?" his pastor asked. The man paused for a moment and responded: "I think that it was that I did not want to fail my Lord Jesus Christ." "But that is only half of it," Dr. Buttrick said. "Your Lord Jesus Christ did not fail you!"

We will experience storms in life. God never promises us that storms will not be there. And he doesn't promise always miraculously to rescue us like this man was delivered from the gangsters. But God is present.

Build For The Long Haul

Start working on the structure of your own life now and build with a long view. Be aware that you are constructing your life through every age — while you are a child, a teenager, a young adult, in middle age, or elderly. You are constantly remaking and shaping your life as you expose yourself to the power of God. Build for the long haul and be able to say, "Rock of ages cleft for me." Remember that Jesus has gone to prepare a place for you, and you want to prepare your life so that you will be worthy, feel familiar and comfortable with the place he has gone to prepare for you.

Build for the long haul. When the storms of life rage around you, with Christ in your life, you will have power within you to sustain you. You will have internal braces that come from the strength of the presence of God to withstand whatever comes. A woman who had undergone some difficult days had a friend turn to her and ask: "How can you stand all of this turmoil and difficulties through which you are going?" "Oh, it's okay," she responded. "The chaos is around me and not within me."

When you have your roots deep in Christ and you are firmly built on the rock foundation of his presence, no matter what storms beat upon your life, you can stand it. When Jesus concluded the Sermon on the Mount, he told about contrast and choices that people have. In one of these choices, he described a way that was broad which leads to destruction. And he said, many will take it. But there is a narrow way, and few will find it. He also described two trees. Each producing fruit according to its own nature. Then he described two houses — one whose foundation was weak and which was swept away by the storms that beat down on it. The other house whose foundation was built on a rock could withstand the storms. Jesus tells us that the choice is up to us. How do you choose?

How Do You Listen?

(Parabke of the Four Soils)

Matthew 13:3-9; 18-23

Jesus sat in a boat a few feet from the shore. A large crowd of people had gathered nearby to hear him. But Jesus knew that a large crowd was no indication that his ministry was necessarily successful. He was not that vain nor naive. He was no longer permitted to preach in the synagogues, so he turned to the open country. Although crowds gathered around him, the scribes and Pharisees were hostile toward Jesus. They could not understand why he broke the sabbath laws, why he did not fast as they did, or why he associated with sinners. They held him in contempt and raised serious questions about his behavior and teachings.

Sitting in the boat, Jesus began to tell the crowd a parable. Nearby on a hillside there may have been a farmer sowing seed. We do not know. That scene was familiar to them anyway. The farmer would probably have his outer garment pulled up into a sack-like shape which held the seed he would use, or he would have a basket in his arm and broadcast the seed from it. In telling a parable about a sower sowing seed, Jesus was not interested in agricultural reform. This was one of seven parables in the thirteenth chapter of the gospel of Matthew on the kingdom of God. This parable really serves as a preface to the other parables about the kingdom of God. The focus in this parable is on hearing. What Jesus is saying to those in the crowd is: "Pay attention now. Listen!" "Take heed therefore how you hear." Later he will say, "He that hath ears to hear, let him hear."

The Sower

Although the main emphasis in this parable is not on the sower, let's take a moment and look at the one who broadcasts the seed. Jesus is most probably giving an autobiographical reference here. He himself is the sower who broadcasts the seed about the kingdom of God. But Jesus was not the kind of sower that the people had anticipated in their image of the Messiah. He was not a militant figure. He did not come as a conqueror. He came as a teacher who sought to persuade and draw people to God, not by coercion but by love, understanding, and compassion. As the sower, he broadcasted his seed everywhere. He let it fall wherever it would so that any who wanted could respond. He practiced what some have called "divine carelessness."

The Seed

What is the seed that is being broadcast? A description of the seed is found in the brief parable found in Mark 14: 26-29. It declares: "The kingdom of God is as if a man should cast seed upon the ground." The image of the sowing of the seed, according to Robert Farrar Capon, depicts the seed of the kingdom of God as being "sown in this world, squarely in the midst of every human and even every earthly condition. This emphasis on the kingdom as a worldly, not just an otherworldly piece of business was already clear in the sower."[34] The proclamation is heralded that the kingdom of God is planted in our world, and the response to that message is determined by the kind of soil in which it falls. We "plant" the seed and leave the response to the hearer. We can't control the reception.

The Soil, The Hard Pathway

The major focus in this parable, however, is on the soil. Four different kinds of soils are mentioned. Jesus began by speaking about seed falling on the wayside soil. This is the soil which had become hard because people trampled over it and turned it into a path. Jeremias and other biblical scholars have stated that in ancient Palestine, the seed was broadcast first before the field was plowed. What might appear to us to be bad farming was

---

34 Robert Farrar Capon, *The Parables of the Kingdom* (Grand Rapids, Michigan: William B. Eerdmans Publishing Co., 1985), 90.

simply a common practice in that day.[35] There were no fences in ancient Palestine, and even if a path were plowed, people would continue to walk over their familiar pathway and make the soil hard very quickly. The seed could not penetrate the hard soil, or if it had been plowed under, it could not come up through the hard surface. The hard pathway represents those who hear the word but do not understand it.

We know something about not being able to understand or comprehend, don't we? We sometimes say that a word goes in one ear and out the other. Or what somebody says simply bounces off our mind or goes over our head and we do not get it. The way some people react to the gospel message, one would think that it was like trying to explain nuclear physics to a small child. The child is simply too young to comprehend the subject, and so the teachings go over her head.

Some of us may simply be out of tune with the message. We can't see it, sense it, or appreciate it. The message passes by us, but we miss it. Several years ago, I had an opportunity to go to the Speed Museum and see the special display of the Armand Hammer paintings. As I walked through the crowded lines of people and looked at the paintings, I listened to some people to hear their observations and comments on the paintings. Many could not appreciate them at all. They had come only out of curiosity. They would look at the painting, and then look at each other and giggle and walk away. There has to be some artistic appreciation to grasp what the artist is trying to say. On the other hand, I noticed others, who would stand before a painting and study it for a long time. They were absorbed by what the artist was trying to depict. They were open and responsive.

Some of us are like the hard path where the seed fell and could not grow. Our minds and hearts are hard and closed, and God's word cannot penetrate them. The scribes and Pharisees were in this group. No matter what Jesus said, they could not hear it. They already had God's word defined and confined. They were not open to new insights or direction from it.

---

35 Joachim Jeremias, The Parables of Jesus (London: SCM Press, 1954), 9-10.

But do not judge those ancient Pharisees too quickly because you and I may be the contemporary Pharisees. We are those who often have our minds closed, our hearts rigid, and God has a difficult time getting any new insight or perspective into our lives. God is contained within our creeds and interpretations, and we are not open to a new word, challenge, or inspiration.

I wonder how many times God has sought to penetrate the minds of those of us who are like a hard path? These people may have heard the gospel many times, but its message simply goes over their head, or their mind wanders, or they do not listen. They have attended church services often or occasionally, or they have gone to funerals or weddings where they have heard the word of God, but it does not penetrate their lives. Why? Well, some are just preoccupied with other things. Religion is of no real consequence to them. They have hardened their lives by indifference. To others, religion has become routine, traditional, and automatic and now no new insights or freshness of the gospel can come into their lives. For others, sin has taken control of a person's life, and he or she has become hardened to God's "voice." They no longer respond to his love. Self-centeredness dominates their life, and their concern is only with self and what they can get from others for themselves. But remember that the path was not always hard. At one time in their life, the soil was rich and fertile. Time has made the pathway of their mind hard, and now it is difficult for them to hear.

When our heart becomes hard, and God's word cannot penetrate our mind, then the parable warns us that the birds will come along and pick up the seed on the hard path. The problem is not simply that we have become hardened to God. When the path is hard, seed that falls on it is also eaten by the birds. Jesus said the birds are symbolic of the satanic power in our lives. What are the birds that peck away at the seed on your hard path? Are they greed, lust, ambition, or power? Name your own! The birds are other forces in our lives which keep the Word of God from germinating in us. As Luther said; "We can't stop the birds from flying over our heads, but we must take heed lest they build their nests in our hair." In St. Paul's Cathedral, there is a bronze tablet on the wall in memory of Canon Samuel A. Barnett who served in east London for many years. A figure of a sower is carved on the tablet. Underneath the image are the words, "Fear not to sow on account of the birds." Life is filled with failures, problems, and burdens. But the seeds need to be sown, whether the birds are there or not.

Rocky Soil

Secondly, Jesus said that the mind of the hearers is like rocky soil. This soil is composed of a thin layer of dirt over rocks. The shallow layer of soil does not have enough depth for the roots to survive. The seed breaks through the ground and looks like for a moment that it has life, but when the sun comes out, the young growth is scorched and soon disappears.

You have seen the people which this soil represents. Preacher X comes along, and they get so excited about the gospel. They are thrilled with it. They give their lives to God and go racing off in service for him. These people are often "converted" at every revival. But their religion is short-lived. They are summertime Christians. When everything is bright and beautiful, they are full of sparkle and life. But when the winter snows and cold winds of life beat down upon them and the difficulties, frustrations, and hardships come, they fall away. They want religion only when it is bright and beautiful, exciting, and thrilling. Their religion is primarily emotional. It is based on how they feel toward God and toward the preacher. If Preacher Y says something they don't like, they pick up their marbles and walk away to another church that thrills them. They have no sense of faithfulness or lasting commitment to God. When some of those in the crowds around Jesus heard his message, they exclaimed: "Lord, I will follow you wherever you go." They were filled with enthusiasm and eager to begin. But Jesus reminded them. "The foxes have holes for a home but the Son of Man has no place to lay his head." Our Lord cautioned those who would follow him to realize the costly nature, the sacrifice, and faithfulness which would be demanded of them if they were to follow him.

In *Bunyan's Pilgrim's Progress*, there is a character called Pliable. Pliable is quickly attracted and becomes excited about traveling with Christian to the Celestial City. He likes the conversation about the seraphim, the cherubim, and the harps of gold. But when he arrives at the Slough of Despond, it is too hard for him and he turns back and returns to the City of Destruction. Later in the City of Destruction, Pliable began to bad-mouth Christian and point out how foolish he thought he was.

The sun easily scorches the new shoots in the rocky soil, because they do not have enough roots. This soil represents shallow and superficial religion. In the young church, superficial Christians fell away quickly when persecution came. In the heat of the day, they withered away. They received the good news with joy, but when they were called upon in crisis to stand up for Christ, their religious roots were shallow and they fell away. Paul's words about Demas: "He has forsaken me," describes these Christians. This parable calls you to get away from shallow religion and instead to dig your roots deep into the soil of Jesus Christ. Genuine religion does not feed us Pablum. When our roots are deep within the soil of the word, we know we are undergirded by the power of God which will sustain us.

Thorny Ground

But some of the seed, Jesus said, also fell on thorny ground. This ground was rich with possibilities. It was fertile. But as farmers say: "It was dirty soil." This soil contained not only the seeds of the farmer's crop within it, but the seeds of thistles and brambles. They grew up along with his planting. Because the field had so many weeds and briars in it, the crop was chocked out and could not grow. Sometimes the weeds in our lives choke out the good things that we could have from God. Our lives get so crowded that there is not enough space for the vitality of life that God wants to bring in our lives. His rich crop is crowded out with other things.

Sometimes we even let good things crowd out the best. All of life is filled with choices. You have to choose what television show you will watch, or what book you will read. If you go to a movie, you have to decide what movie you will see. You have to choose daily, sometimes hourly, what you will do with your time. You have to decide what you will eat, what you will wear, and where you will go. Sometimes our choices are vain and foolish. We need to learn to choose the best and not just the good. Unfortunately, we often let good things crowd out the best. We are preoccupied but not with the best.

Fertile fields can be strangled by weeds and thistles. Jesus said that these thorns might be "the cares of the world," or "the deceitfulness of riches." Our motives are often mixed with conflicting hopes and frustrations, dreams and anxieties, generosity and selfishness, and faith and doubt. Do not let the thorns crowd out the seed of God which is seeking to find growth in your life.

The Good Soil

Jesus concluded this parable by saying that some of the seed fell on good soil. When it fell on the good soil, it found the soil rich, sent its roots down deep, and it immediately sprang to life. The main emphasis of this parable is on the good soil. In this parable Jesus is not focusing on fatalism, despair or defeat in sowing the seed, but he is stressing the positive results that come from seed being planted in good soil. When it falls on good soil, he notes that it brings forth fruit a hundred, sixty, or thirty-fold. Although the sowing of the seed is often difficult and it cannot grow everyplace, it will bring forth a rich vital crop in good soil.

That is a word we all need to hear today. It is easy to give in to despair and cynicism and wonder if there is any point to our labor. There are times when the sowing is so difficult that we don't want to try any longer. We become discouraged and want to throw up our hands and quit. Some have said: "If I thought the rest of my efforts were going to be like what's happening to me now, I would just walk away from it." In the light of your struggle, you might want to say: "Well, I'm not doing much good. I might as well quit."

Jesus reminds us in this parable that every effort has the possibility of reaping some crop when it is sown. This is a great word of encouragement. All of the seed may not find soil for growth, but some will. That's the important point. This parable celebrates hope and not failure.

The Nature Of Good Soil

What is the nature of the good soil of a hearer? He or she is attentive, open, receptive, responsive, and obedient to God. The soil of our heart lies open and receptive. And when the seed of God is planted, new life springs out of our soil.

People who have undergone heart by-pass surgery are aware that their heart is stopped during the operation. After the operation is completed, an electric spark is used to start the heart beating again. God reaches into our life and "touches" our heart to start it beating in a new way. As we open our lives to him, the power of his presence revitalizes us. The New Covenant which we receive from Jesus Christ is a fulfillment of the one promised by Jeremiah when he prophesied: "Behold the days are coming says the Lord, when I will make a new covenant with the house of Israel and the house of Judah. I will put my law within them, and I will write it upon their hearts; and I will be their God, and they shall be my people" (Jeremiah 31:31-33). The vitality, the newness of life, the new birth which God can give to us is an encouraging word. It is a word that offers to us hope in a time of difficulty.

I think there is a real difference between appreciating and affirming a person. We often appreciate people because they demonstrate that they have certain gifts. They may play the organ, the piano, or sing, and we appreciate them for their gifts. But we affirm a person for who he or she is. Even if a person's gifts are small or none, we can affirm and encourage them. This parable is an encouraging word for all who work in the cause of Christ.

Plant Your Seeds Where You Are

Listen to its sounds of hope. Some of you have taught Sunday school for years and wonder if you ever do any good. Jesus is reminding you that the seed you plant may fall on fertile soil and bring forth a far richer crop than you could ever imagine. I wonder if some of my Sunday school teachers questioned the good they were doing when they taught that mischievous teenager. I can remember the Sunday school teacher I had who did not know how to read. But he taught a group of teenage boys each week. Out of Mr. Martin's Sunday school class came two ministers. It is easy to become discouraged in Christian work.

Many people have struggled with discouragement. Vincent van Gogh was so depressed that he took his own life. He felt his paintings were unappreciated and of little value. He has been dead almost a hundred years now, and recently one of his paintings sold for forty million dollars. William Carey labored for years in India before a single soul was converted. But he continued to preach and teach during that time. Frederick W. Robertson thought he was a failure as a minister and was deeply depressed in his years as a minister. Today he is recognized as one of the greatest preachers of the nineteenth century. We cannot judge properly our own success or failures. What we are called upon to do is to sow the seed. We sow the seed and leave the harvest to God. We never know what good may come from seeds we have planted. There have been times when I have preached that I have thought: "Boy, this was sure a bomb today." Then someone would drop a note, or telephone, or say a word to indicate that something I said was helpful, gave them a new insight, or guided them along a path during a difficult time. We simply never know.

A man in India picked up a scrap of paper which was a page torn from a New Testament. On this scrap of paper was the selection from John 3:16. This man knew that this quotation came from the book of the Christians. He went to a tiny mission in his town and inquired: "Is this really true?" That piece of paper changed his life. It was a tiny seed that changed his life.

As you assist in the nursery, work with small children, teenagers, or adults, you never know the results that may come from the seeds you plant. They may reap a great harvest for God. Reach out to a neighbor in need. Help with a flood or hurricane victim. Visit the sick; encourage a friend; babysit for a young mother; listen to a friend's problems or grief; offer a person a ride to the doctor. Let us sow the seeds with joy. Though we may never see all of the results of our work, let us trust in God to bring his own harvest in his own good time. Although the seed may seem fragile and vulnerable, it is amazingly tough. There is great power in the seed. As Christian disciples, we are responsible for sowing the seed and pointing others to God. We sow and then trust.

Which Kind Of Soil Are We?

Now remember before you try to decide which one of these soils might be representative of you, it might be best to point out that they are four possible characteristics of your heart and mine. At times, we may be any one of them. There are occasions that you are like the wayside path and your life is very hard and God has a great difficulty trying to penetrate your mind with a new thought. There are times that you are rocky soil and religion for you is mainly excitement. You are conscious that your roots are not very deep and you are shallow and need to grow spiritually. There are other times that weeds crowd Christ out of your life. Everything else is more important. Work to make your soil rich so God can plant the seed of his presence deep in the soil of your life. Don't confine God to the crannies, cracks, and narrow places of your heart and mind. Let him have full opportunity to cultivate the soil of your life. Lie open and responsive to his spirit.

In the deserts of Arizona, a man lived in a small cabin on the edge of the wasteland. He had the only well of water in the entire area. Each night he would hang a lantern high outside his cabin, just in case somebody might be lost in the desert and needed to find water. Many thought he was foolish to waste oil this way. One night he was awakened by a faint knock at the door. He opened the door and a man fell exhausted at his feet. He had become lost in the desert. He had seen the light shining faintly at a distance, and he continued to walk toward it until he found the cabin and received water. A man's life was saved because an old man cared enough to hang a lantern on his cabin each night in case someone was in need.

We are called to hold up the light of Christ and to let it shine in a world filled with darkness. Wherever the seeds from that light may fall, we let God, in his own time and way, grow the crop within the soil of our heart. Learn to listen as you remain open, receptive, responsive, and obedient to the word that comes from God.

Does It Do Any Good To Pray?

(Parable of the Friend Coming at Midnight)

Luke 11:5-13

"I can't believe in God anymore," the woman said. "I prayed to him when my husband had cancer. I asked that he be spared. But he did nothing. Any decent person would have helped. God was only silent, so I can no longer believe in him." This woman reflects the feeling of many who feel that God at times has been silent to their requests. Their voices rose to heaven, but there seemed to be no ear to hear, and no response to the requests which came to God.

How are we to respond to this kind of dilemma regarding prayer? A part of our problem arises from the way men and women see God. Some see God as the manager of an eternal insurance company where he is supposed to protect them from every loss, bruise, possible injury, hurt, catastrophe, or illness which they might experience. Others see God as the proprietor of a lost and found department, where they can reclaim lost hours, lost opportunities, or other abandoned treasures along life's pathway. Still others see God as the divine insomniac, who is always awake to prevent them from hurting themselves or making a wrong turn or taking a forbidden path. Still others view God as the keeper of an eternal fountain of youth where they can come and drink again from his stream, and God will restore their misspent youth or abused middle age. What kind of concept of prayer do we have if we perceive God in this light?

A Perspective On Prayer

Our scripture text offers us a perspective on prayer. We observe that Jesus had been praying in a certain place. His disciples, who had seen the continuous example of his praying and noted the power which prayer made in his life, came to him one day and asked: "Master, teach us to pray." We do not know whether their request was primarily that Jesus teach them a prayer which they could pray, since what you and I call The Lord's Prayer follows. On the other hand, the disciples may have been asking Jesus to teach them how to pray. In this gospel, Jesus responds to their request by giving three parables. Here we shall examine one of them — the parable about the man who came at midnight and requested help from a friend.

This parable is the story about a man who had a friend call upon him unexpectedly late at night. At midnight, the host called upon a friend to ask him for three loaves of bread. In that age, people went to bed early and got up when the sun came up. When the host came calling at night, his friend's family was already in bed. It was the Eastern tradition that the door to a person's house was left open in the daytime. When a door was open, that was a sign that anyone was welcome. But when the door was shut at night, the message was clear: "We don't want to be disturbed by anybody!" It was also much more inconvenient to visit someone at night then than it is today. Their houses were modestly small, usually only one room. The dirt floors were covered with dried rushes and reeds. The floor usually had two levels. At nighttime, the family would bring the cattle, hens, and other livestock into the lower level to keep them safe from thieves. At the back side of the house, there was a raised level where the family slept on mats — not beds as we have today. The family would sleep close together, particularly if the weather were cold. They slept near a small brazier and covered themselves with rugs to keep warm at night. With this kind of sleeping arrangement, the father would literally disturb everybody — his wife, his children, and the animals — if he got up to respond to his friend's request. "Don't bother me. The door is shut," he cried. "Any idiot can see that! Don't disturb me now."

But the midnight friend knew his neighbor well, and he kept beating on the door. He knew that this guy was all talk but deep down inside he was a real softie. So, he continued knocking on the door and finally, not out of friendship, Jesus notes, but because the man doesn't want to be shamed, he gets up to give his neighbor some assistance. Everybody in the east was by custom supposed to be a good neighbor. If he didn't get up, he would be shamed because he was being un-neighborly. The sleepy man finally gets up and gives his late-calling neighbor what he needs. This is an interesting, yet strange — humorous, tragic, and in some ways, difficult parable. Remember no one parable contains all the truth about God. This parable does not address every aspect of prayer. It only gives us one dimension. Let's see if we can possibly discover what that truth is.

Why We Should Pray

Well, for one thing, I think the parable teaches us something about why we should pray. The host went to his neighbor, his friend, for some food, because he had a need which he could not meet by himself. He had come to the end of his own resources. A friend had come in the middle of the night to visit him. He did not have enough bread to take care of his friend who had come unexpectedly to see him. His cupboard was bare. So, he went to the home of a neighbor to get some assistance.

A Sense Of Need

One of the reasons we pray is out of a sense of need. Now, remember this is not the only dimension of prayer, but we are seeking to understand the lesson of this parable. We often pray out of our own awareness of our need. We come to the realization sometimes that our resources, our own strength, are not sufficient to face everything in life. We come to the end of the rope of our own self-sufficiency, and we turn to God. We come to the dead-end streets of our own confusions, and we look for a new thoroughfare which God can provide. We find that the waves of doubts, fears, frustrations, and anxieties swamp our own small craft. We cry out that we are sinking, and we turn to God. Our load, our burdens crush us down and become too heavy to bear, and we reach up to find resources beyond ourselves to sustain us. That power is God. Sometimes we pray because we honestly realize our own resources are inadequate.

In many of the psalms, a voice is raised expressing frustration, confusion, or anxiety in knowing where God is in the writer's hour of need. "Why is my soul cast down?" A psalmist asked. "I will hope in the Lord." Jeremiah cried in his moment of rejection and isolation, "I sat alone." There was no one who seemed to care about him or his problem. He wondered where God was in his hour of desperation. "I prayed three times that God would remove my thorn from my flesh," Paul noted, "but each time, God's silence seems to imply 'my grace is sufficient.'" In the Garden of Gethsemane Jesus cried, "O God, if it is possible, let this cup pass from me." But it did not pass, and he drank it, dregs and all.

But you know what it is like to approach God in your own time of need. You have a baby who has been sick, and you have felt completely helpless. Your wife or husband has cancer, and you can only stand by and watch, knowing that you can do nothing. You have had to place a parent or child in some institution for help. Your marriage seems to be falling apart; your children are uncontrollable; your parents do not understand you; or you have lost your job. You have experienced loneliness, depression, anxiety, and fear, and you did not know where to turn for help. You have been pushed to the end of your own resources, and the only place you feel you can turn is to God. Our need sometimes gives a voice to our prayers. Prayer rises from our heart as a spontaneous expression of a deep need or desire in our heart.

Assured A Friend Will Respond

But notice another dimension of why we should pray. The neighbor went to a friend, because he knew that he would help him. He had a friend to whom he could turn. Although it was late, he did not hesitate to knock on his door. He continued to pound on it until his friend answered. The parable indicates that his friend did not help him out of friendliness, but assisted him because he did not want to be put to shame. Some translations have rendered this phrase as "because of his importunity" but literally it should read "shamelessness." Some translations render this word as "persistence." But literally the words may be rendered: "He did not want to be put to shame." To stop his neighbor from bothering him at this late hour, he responded.

Contrasting With God

We make a mistake if we think that Jesus is telling us that God is like this man, who did not want to be awakened by his neighbor. He makes a contrast instead of drawing a likeness. God is not asleep and must be awakened to meet our needs. God doesn't say, "Quit bothering me with your silly requests. I am not interested in them at this hour. Can't you see I am trying to rest?" We don't have to nag him until we finally get his attention, and then God reluctantly responds so we will stop bothering him. Jesus gives us our key to the mystery when he said that, although this man assisted his neighbor for the wrong reason, "how much more;" "how much more," "*how much more*" will our heavenly Father give us? There is the clue! Jesus reasoned from the worst to the best, from the lesser to the higher to show the kind of response that God makes compared to a human father. An earthly father will not give his children something that will harm them. If a child asks for fish to eat, his father doesn't give him a snake that might hurt him. If he asks for an egg, he doesn't give him a scorpion that might bite him. If your human father understands your needs, how much more does God understand and care?

How To Pray:
Approach God Personally

Secondly, the parable tells us something about how to pray. Notice that the host came personally to his neighbor's house. He knocked on the door and made his request known personally to him. You and I can pray to God personally, Thank goodness! We don't have to pray through a priest, a pastor, or someone else. We can go personally and directly to God, who personally responds to us. God is not the first cause or divine principle. He is personal, Jesus called God Father. He is the eternal friend, the one we know we can turn to and be assured he will listen in times of need.

Make A Specific Request

We also see that the host had specific requests which he made of his neighbor. He didn't go and babble as he stood outside his neighbor's door and give him a dissertation on the importance of meals. He asked for three loaves of bread. What he was really saying in the eastern tradition was, "I don't have a knife, fork, and spoon for my unexpected friend and I need them to provide him a meal." Bread was literally used in ancient time like a knife, fork, and spoon. A piece of bread would be broken off in a bite size and then dipped in a common dish, and afterward it would be eaten. Following that, a fresh piece of bread would be broken off and dipped in the common dish and then eaten. And this pattern would continue through the meal. "Give me some bread," the host asked. "Give me a knife, fork, and spoon." It was a very simple, modest request, but a very particular one.

You and I sometimes wonder why our prayers are never answered. Too often we pray: "God bless all the missionaries everywhere, all the preachers, all the doctors, all the teachers, and all the churches." We need to learn to let our prayers be more particularized. Be specific! Pray, "God bless this church; this individual in a concrete way; or help this person with her particular burden; help me with my load; help my child in this way or another." Move from generalities to being very particular in your prayer focus.

Be Persistent

Notice further that the host was persistent in his request of his neighbor. He didn't knock on the door and the first time the neighbor said, "I'm sorry, I'm asleep now," then he turned and left. He continued to knock on the door. He persisted until his neighbor responded. Sometimes a person asks, "Why do I have to keep on telling God something? He knows what my needs are. Why should I tell him again and again?" I am convinced that one of the reasons we have a need for persistence in prayer is that it tests whether we are serious about our request. Is this just a casual request we are bringing to God? Is my desire to have this request granted so urgent that I know it will have a long-term effect on my life, family, and whatever I am involved in? Or is my request something which I might like to have, if possible? Is it an urgent need? Is there an insistence on your part that seems to border on presumption to ask for such a thing? Why should we expect God to answer our prayers unless there is evidence in our life that our prayers are earnest and sincere? All worthwhile goals in life are reached by disciplined efforts. Why should we expect less in our prayer efforts?

The scriptures indicate that Jesus sometimes prayed all night long. Why didn't he pray: "Father, you know I really have a heavy burden now? I have a tough day tomorrow. Help me." Why did he wrestle all night long in prayer? "Pray without ceasing." Paul wrote. I believe that prayer affects more the individual who prays than it does God. We pray with persistence to open ourselves to God so that he can find an avenue into our own lives to give us direction and strength.

A Call For Patience

The scripture writers charge repeatedly: "Wait, wait on the Lord." What does it mean to say, "Wait on the Lord?" Well, I think one of the things it means is that we have to learn to be more patient. God doesn't always grant everything just like we want it. He sees your life and his world in a longer, wider perspective. God sees the whole picture, so wait on the Lord. Will B. Dunn is a preacher in a comic strip which Doug Marlette draws. In one of his cartoons, Will B. Dunn is pictured on his knees praying, "Please, Lord, give me patience!" In the next scene, while still on his knees, he is looking at his watch. Then in the final scene he looks up and says, "Well?"

That is an indication of how quickly we want God to respond. We make a request of God, days pass, and time drags on. God has not answered our request as quickly as we have wanted. "Well," we ask God, "What are you doing?" We haven't learned to wait on the Lord with humility, patience, faith, reverence, and hope. Our reactions seem to be, "Well, I have made my request. How come you haven't responded as I have asked you, O Lord?" We don't really know what it means to wait on the Lord, do we?

A small girl was kneeling by her bed, saying her prayers. When she finished her prayers, she lingered on her knees by her bed for what seemed a long period of time to her mother. As she got up, she explained to her mother, "I was waiting to see if God had anything to say to me." Ah, sometimes children can teach us some valuable lessons, can't they? We are so busy making our request — no, our demands of God — that we don't listen. Can you believe our pompous attitude? Here we are, frail children of dust, as the scriptures describe us, and we demand that the eternal God of the universe give us whatever we want instantly in our way and time. The audacity of this attitude is staggering.

What Kind Of Response Do You Expect?
This parable also gives us an opportunity to observe what kind of response you can expect from your prayers. It is clear that the host did expect a response from his neighbor. The host went at night to his neighbor's house and continued pounding on the door until his neighbor got up and answered his request. He persisted until he got a response. It is not clear exactly what he did receive. The parable states clearly that the neighbor got up and met his friend's needs. We don't know if he got the three loaves which he requested or if he got more provisions than he solicited. If the neighbor gave his friend some meat or other food items, the parable does not disclose it. Jesus simply states that the neighbor met his friend's need.

God does respond to our prayers. Sometimes his response is: "No way, brother or sister!" God looks at the effect his response will have on the total direction of your life and on the course of history itself. God's response to you does not affect you alone but the whole universe. Can you expect God to set aside all the laws of the universe so you can have your way?

Think about the many requests which are made of God. Some of our prayers are vain, foolish, ridiculous, and selfish. It is difficult for us to realize that God often responds by saying no to our request. But his denial is still a response. A small boy, in *Children's Letters To God*, writes: "Dear God, I wrote you before, do you remember? Well, I did what I promised. But you did not send me the horse yet. What about it?" Signed Lewis.[36] A lot of us pray just like Lewis. "Okay God, I asked you for that Rolls Royce. Where is it? What about it?"

But do the scriptures not declare: "Ask and you will receive. Knock and it will be opened. Seek and you will find"? Knock, ask, seek. I had a woman tell me one time, "The scriptures say, 'Ask and you will receive.' That is the reason I have asked for this item. Because I asked, I know I will get it!" Well, Jesus did say that. How are we to understand exactly what he said? Some interpreters say that we should take these statements at face value. You can ask God for anything and expect to receive it. Since Jesus said, "ask," God has to give you what you request. But think for a moment. We know that Jesus himself didn't get every prayer answered as he personally requested. When he was in the Garden of Gethsemane, he prayed: "Lord, let this cup pass from me. I don't want this." But he did have to drink it. Just because he asked for it to pass, did not in fact make it happen. Jesus said to his disciples on another occasion. "Whatsoever you shall ask in my name, that will I do."

Ah, there is the difference, isn't it? The emphasis is, "In my name." This doesn't mean that you merely quote the name, "Jesus." "In my name" means in the spirit of Jesus. "In my name" is Jesus' way of saying that whatever someone asks of God has to be according to his will, according to his ministry, according to what he was seeking to achieve, and according to the purpose of the kingdom of God. Jesus prayed, "Not my will but thine be done." The Greek verb forms of "ask, seek, and knock" are present imperatives. The literal meaning is "keep on asking," "keep on seeking," and "keep on knocking." The statement means be habitual, be persistent, don't be discouraged, continue faithfully in your request of God. Some further help on seeking to understanding God's response to our prayers is offered in my book, *Lord, I Keep Getting a Busy Signal: Reaching for a Better Spiritual Connection*.[37]

---

36 Eric Marshall and Stuart Hample (Compilers), *Children's Letters to God* (New York: An Essandess Special edition, 1967), 23.
37 William Powell Tuck, *Lord I Keep Getting a Busy Signal: Reaching for a Better Spiritual Connection* (Gonzales, FL: Energion Publications, 2014).

How Much More

The clue to understanding how God responds to our prayer requests seems to me to be answered in verse thirteen of the parable where Jesus stated, "How much more shall your Heavenly Father give the Holy Spirit to those who ask him." Jesus doesn't say that you will always get what you want or that you will get "things" which you request. What you receive from God is the best gift of all. You receive God's presence — his Spirit. You may not receive things in answer to your prayers. You may not get exactly what you want, but your need will be met, nevertheless. The neighbor in the parable requested three loaves of bread from his friend to provide food for his unexpected guest. His request was not to get something for himself, but to meet another's needs.

Ultimately, what you and I ask of God must be in accordance with God's will. Our request needs to be in accordance to what will advance God's kingdom. If God grants your request, will it help his cause and not merely feed your ego, make you look better in some light, or make you richer? I do not believe that Jesus has told us: "Ask anything, and you will get it." He did not mean, "Ask what you want and you will become richer, more glamorous, or famous." "Ask," Jesus states, "and you will receive the Holy Spirit." Our prayers are to be asked "in his name," and "according to God's will."

The emphasis on persistence is not simply to encourage us to nag God until he responds. We do not pound on a closed door of an empty house. Jesus clearly indicates in other places that God is available and accessible. As our eternal friend, God is caring, loving, and responsive. We pray without ceasing so we may be open to sense God's will, way, purpose, and goals in the world. We pray persistently that our will may become merged in his will.

In a practical sense, persistence in prayer will enable you to forget your own desires until they are absorbed in God's will. Persistence in prayer can lead us away from seeking specific "things" and into deeper communion with God. Do you remember the story where Jacob agonized with God in prayer? After Jacob wrestled all night with God, he finally asked: "Tell me what is your name?" What Jacob's persistent request seemed to mean was: "Expose your presence to me." As you open yourself to God in prayer through persistence, hopefully selfish goals will lessen and your desire will become more to be one with him and that his will might be your will. Persistence in prayer may lead you to realize that this world and the material things in it are not the ultimate values and ends in life. To expose yourself to God through prayer is to open yourself to the spiritual realm which begins in this world, but stretches into eternity. "This is eternal life," John wrote, "to know the son." To have fellowship with God here begins a relationship which stretches from the physical world into the spiritual realm, and continues after death.

John Sherrill, a noted journalist, wrote about his experience when he first became a Christian and the impact his Christian community had on him as he grew in his relationship to God. He told about an experience he had one time with another member of the church choir of which he was a member. One of the members of the choir had a breathtaking bass voice which was rich in its beauty and depth. He sat in front of this man in the choir and felt that his ability to sing was greatly enriched by that great voice behind him. One night he expressed appreciation to his friend for his beautiful voice, and he told him how much it helped him in his own singing. "Tonight, in choir practice," his friend replied, "I want you to lean back on me while we are singing and see the difference that will make." That night, during the rehearsal, his friend with the powerful voice, urged him to lean back on him. As he did, he felt the power of his friend's voice penetrate his own body. His own voice swelled and was more powerful than it had ever been.

Persistence in prayer enables us to merge ourselves into God. We lean upon God in our prayers in order that his breath — his spirit — might penetrate and permeate our inner being and influence all that we are and do. Yes, it makes a difference whether you and I pray. Oh, we may not always get everything we want, but, if we pray persistently, we will get the most important gift of all — the presence of God. And that, my friends, is enough!

Squirming In The Net Of Judgment

(Parable of the Dragnet)

Matthew 13:47-48

"It seems so contradictory. It's out of focus for what the church ought to be," the pastor said. "The work is too frustrating. Everywhere I have turned I have met church members who have discouraged me, betrayed the teachings of Christ, and compromised the gospel to have their own way. I am going to quit. There is no point in trying. I came into the ministry with such high goals and dreams, but the church simply falls short." What minister has not felt like that?

"I'm not going to church again," the woman thundered. "It is full of hypocrites." And it is! A deacon from a leading church in his community was arrested and sent to jail because he had stolen funds from the business where he worked. I read about a treasurer of a church who was arrested because he had stolen money from his church.

What are we to make of such words and actions by people within the church? I think the parable from Matthew 13 that Jesus told about the dragnet touches on some aspects of this problem. Let's examine this parable and see if it offers us some guidance.

A Parable Fishermen Would Grasp

Many of the first disciples who followed Jesus were fishermen. Jesus instructed them to look at their own workaday world and draw a parable about the kingdom of heaven from it. Fishermen would often row two boats out onto the lake of Galilee and drop a large net between the boats. The net was usually square with large corks at each corner and heavy weights were attached to the bottom of the net. The weights would force the net to stand up in the water. Ropes were tied to the corners of the net. As the boat slowly moved through the water, the net gradually took on a cone shape and captured everything in its path. The fishermen would pull the net into their boats with their catch. From this catch, they selected the good fish and discarded the bad. According to the Leviticus law (Leviticus 11:9-12), the Jewish people could eat only fish with fins and scales. This meant that all the other things they caught in the sea, they had to discard. Jesus warned his disciples that one day all people will stand before God the Father and at that time the good will be separated from the bad. For some, this will be a time of joy. For others, it will be a time of weeping and gnashing of teeth. Now what does such a parable mean?

The Meaning Of The Net

The net, I believe, represents the kingdom of God and its influence in the world, and the church is the earthly manifestation of that kingdom. Jesus is saying that the kingdom of heaven or the kingdom of God is like a net that sweeps through all the world to draw men and women to God. The church is the instrument of the kingdom which reaches into the world to proclaim the news of God's grace, to teach men and women who are in the kingdom, and to train and provide them opportunities for service. The church cannot be identified with the kingdom of God. They are not the same. The kingdom of God is far more inclusive and wider in its scope than the church. But the church is the realm of redemption through which God works to bring people to him. The kingdom is larger than the church; it is the fellowship of believers. The kingdom of God is the invisible net of God's reign which stretches across all of humanity where his Spirit is always seeking to expose people to his power and presence.

God's Net Gathers All

Moment by moment, hour by hour, day by day, and year by year, people are being drawn into that invisible net. It is God who draws the net tighter and tighter. Daily God judges us, but there will be a final day when the net will be gathered to shore and God will judge its contents. Just as Jesus gathered disciples by his preaching in parables, his disciples will gather men and women into his kingdom by their preaching.

Non-Discriminatory

One of the interesting things about the dragnet is that it takes in all that enters it. The dragnet cannot be selective or discriminating. From its beginning, Jesus founded his church to be inclusive. "God is no respecter of people, but in every nation, he that fears him and works righteousness, is accepted with him" (Acts 10:34-35). The kingdom of heaven is open to any and all people who would commit their lives to Christ and follow him. Jesus sought by words, deeds, and example to draw all people to God. We sometimes forget what a radical teaching this was in the day of Jesus. Barriers of all kinds existed. Separation, segregation, and exclusion were a familiar part of the life in the ancient world.

Barriers Of All Kinds

Look at the Greek world. The Greeks had erected a barrier between themselves and others. If a person was not a Greek, he or she was considered a Barbarian. Barbarians could not speak the beautiful Greek language. We know too well what the word barbarian means. A mother might sometimes say to her child, "Don't act like a barbarian." A barbarian is someone who is uncultured, uncouth, and often wild in his behavior. The Greeks also had established barriers between the slave and the free, the educated and the uneducated.

The Romans also saw themselves as superior to other people. Although they had a high standard for law and justice in their day, they still considered people who were non-Romans as inferior. Do you remember Paul's plea after he was arrested and the Jewish leaders had him put in prison to await trial? He knew his rights as a Roman citizen and said, "I appeal to Caesar." Roman citizens had certain rights that were denied to others.

The Jews probably had the most barriers of all people in the ancient world. The Jews saw everybody else as a Gentile — a person unworthy of God's love. The Jews saw themselves as God's selected people — God's chosen people — which made them superior to all others. Not only were there barriers between Jew and Gentile, but between men and women. A Jewish man got up every morning and thanked God that he was not a Gentile and not a woman. Women were viewed as property of the men. A man could divorce his wife easily if she did not satisfy his absolute wishes. The Jews also made a distinction between those who kept the ceremonial law and those who did not.

Barriers Today

Economic Barriers

In our own day, we have erected barriers of all kinds. There is the economic barrier. Our society is composed of those who are extremely poor and those who are extremely wealthy. Several years ago, when I lived in Kentucky, a survey revealed that 19% of the population lived in poverty; 56% of the families headed by women with preschool children lived in poverty. Approximately 165,000 households in Kentucky depended on food stamps; 48% of these people had incomes below $3,600, and 57% had children under fifteen. It has not improved today. In many of our communities, those who seek to assist the homeless have to turn away two for every one for whom they can provide a place. In our own country and around the world, there is a tremendous economic barrier between those who have and those who have not.

Michael Elliott has written a delightful book entitled *The Society of Salty Saints*. These are people he has met in his innercity ministry at the Jefferson Street Baptist Chapel in Louisville, Kentucky. These people live in a different economic environment than we do. His story is about a bald, elderly woman who chews tobacco, an alcoholic named Bruce, and a woman named Grace. These people and others are the saints who live on "Low Income Boulevard."[38]

There is an ancient story about a scholar named Muretus. Being poor, he wandered from town to town, teaching wherever he could. He fell ill in Italy and was taken to some doctors who thought he was a vagrant. While they were examining him, they spoke in Latin, which was the cultured language of that day. They implied that since he was of no use to anyone, it didn't

---

38 Micheal Elliott, *The Society of Salty Saints* (Oak Park, Indiana, Meyer Stone & Co.).

really matter whether they helped him or not. They saw him as worthless and a nobody. But Muretus looked up at them and spoke in fluent Latin, "Call no one worthless for whom Christ died." All people, no matter what their economic status, are important in God's sight.

Racial Barriers

There are also racial barriers in our world today. The color of a person's skin has caused barriers to separate people from one another. And is still evident in too many ways today. I have often wondered what a difference it would have made in Ghandi's life if, when he went to worship in a white church in South Africa, he had not been turned away because his skin was dark. The image he received of Christianity that day turned him against the institutional church. Christians would not accept him in their church, but he always admired Jesus. Racial barriers unfortunately continue in our world.

Barriers Of Closed Attitudes

There are barriers of perspectives, attitudes, and philosophies which separate us from each other. Some people are totally unwilling to give in at all to another way of thinking. "I know the truth. This is my view, and if you don't agree with it, then you are wrong." We find this in too many arenas in life. These people shut others out because of their perspective. If somebody doesn't agree with this person's view, then that individual is told that he or she has no right to his or her opinion. These people have closed the door to those who differ with them. They are unwilling to listen to another view. Selfishness dominates and clouds their perspective.

You may have heard about two twin brothers, age five, who were surprised on Christmas morning with identical red fire-engine trucks. The father, who was holding Jimmy in his lap, gave him first choice. "Jimmy," the father asked, "which one of these fire engines do you want?" "I want the one John wants," he replied. Too often that is our attitude in life. Whatever somebody else wants is what we want. We want to have our way and force others to accept our view.

Education Barriers And Others

Educational barriers exist. Many in our country are illiterate. They cannot read at all. Others are well educated. These people can read the classics and great books. There are others who are taught primarily by television.

Jesus Shatters Barriers

There are barriers of all kinds that still exist in today's world. Others, of course, could be named. But the message we need to hear is that Jesus Christ came not to erect barriers, but to destroy them. Paul, writing to the Galatian Church, declared: "For there is neither Jew nor Greek, there is neither slave nor free, there is neither male nor female; for you are all one in Christ Jesus" (Galatians 3:28). Jesus Christ came into the world to destroy the walls of exclusion. He demonstrated through his teachings and actions that God is receptive of all people. He crossed sexual lines and reached out to women. He talked to a Samaritan woman at the village well. A rabbi did not talk to a woman in public. That was unheard of in the time of Jesus. It was considered a disgrace! But he did it! He reached out to a woman caught in the act of adultery and forgave her. He ate in the home of two women, Mary and Martha. Women were among his disciples, and they were the first people to come to his tomb on the morning of his resurrection.

Jesus reached out to the wealthy — Joseph of Arimathea, Zacchaeus, and others. He reached out to affluent religious leaders like Nicodemus. He reached out to the poor, the sick, the outcast, the blind, the deaf, the lame, those who were ceremonially unclean, like lepers and harlots, and even Gentiles. He reached out to all people who had a need to hear a word of grace and forgiveness and assured them of God's love and acceptance. He declared, "Those who are well have no need of a physician, but those who are sick" (Matthew 9:12). Jesus knocks at the door of every human heart and whosoever opens can be his disciple. Remember, the Church of Jesus Christ is inclusive. Any person — man or woman, black or white, red or yellow, young or old, rich or poor, educated or unlettered — whosoever will can be his disciple. The ground at the foot of the cross is level. All people are welcomed by him. God's grace and love are available to all.

An Inclusive Church

The church is to be the extension of the incarnation in the world today. We are to be like our Lord as we share his message of love. I like the statement that the city temple in London, England used to carry on its worship bulletin. "To all who are weary and seek rest; to all who mourn and long for comfort; to all who struggle and desire victory; to all who sin and need a Savior; to all who are idle and look for service; to all who are strangers and want fellowship; to all who hunger and thirst after righteousness; and to whosoever will come — this church opens her doors and offers her welcome in the name of Jesus Christ Her Lord." The arms of Christ are extended to all people to come to him. The dragnet reminds us that the Church of Jesus Christ is an inclusive church. Everyone is welcome.

Because the church is inclusive, that means that there will always be a mixture within it. The dragnet reveals a mixed catch. The net brings in all kinds of fish. In his parable about the tares growing in the wheat, Jesus said to "let them both grow together." The church will always be a mixture of good and bad, pure and impure, committed and uncommitted, believers and doubters. But remember that this has always been true of the church. It is simply untrue that the early church was a pure and unblemished church. Look at the disciples of Jesus. They were not without weaknesses and faults. Judas betrayed him. Peter denied him. Thomas always had big questions about religion. The early church was filled with people who were drawn to it for mixed reasons. The Corinthian church was split with all kinds of controversies, divisions, and corruption. Paul wrote to the Philippian church and warned that, "Some of you are enemies of Christ" (Philippians 3:18). Some of the people in the churches were divided in their allegiance to Paul, Apollos, and Peter. When someone states that we should be like the early church, he or she needs to be careful which of the early churches is selected as a model. The early church was sometimes distorted in their beliefs and corrupt in their moral values. They were a mixed bag, just like the church is today.

Churches Are Not Perfect

People of all kinds are drawn into the church. Their motives and reasons are always mixed. Some are good, and some bad, healthy, and unhealthy, genuine and ingenuine. Maybe it would help pastors, deacons, and all church members to realize that the church is an imperfect instrument. The church is not perfect. The church is made up of saints, yes, but these saints are not perfect people. Saints in the biblical understanding of that word are those people who have committed their lives to Christ and are seeking to follow him. They are not perfect individuals. The church is always filled with those who are good and evil, committed and uncommitted, servants and spectators. If you are looking for a perfect church, you need to realize that it doesn't exist.

But we live with imperfection all the time, don't we? If you don't believe so, talk to your wife. Speak to your husband, converse with your children. Ask them to be honest. We know there is imperfection in the home. We can see it clearly there. It's hard to find perfect preachers too, isn't it? They don't exist. Emily loves to tell the story that one of her favorite professors at Meredith College, Dr. Mac, used to tell. There was a preacher who ran off to the next county with the offering from one Sunday morning. He was later caught. "What did you do with him?" the church leaders were asked. "Why," they responded, "we brought him back and made him preach out every cent of it!"

Congregations are not always perfect either. People seem to look for perfect congregations. They want faultless choirs, ideal pastors and teachers, crystal clean cathedrals, an infallible theology, an inerrant Bible, mature teenagers, and model parents. But their ideal view of the church doesn't really exist. The church is filled with imperfections, because there are human beings in it. We have to remember the nature of Christian growth. We do not come into the kingdom of God as a baby, and suddenly we are a full-grown Christian. We are all in process of becoming like Christ. We are continuously in process of maturing, growing, and developing in our spiritual nature. We never arrive.

Several years ago, in a church member's home, he shared with me the minutes from some church business meetings in the rural church where he grew up. There were several occasions where the congregation had "unchurched" some of its members. They had been excommunicated because they had been dancing or drinking. If we unchurched people for those reasons today, we wouldn't have many people left in a lot of our churches. But the notion of excommunicating individuals to have a pure church is foolish. The pure or perfect church doesn't exist.

I heard about a church that continued to excommunicate all of its members which were not pure Christians. Finally, the church had only a husband and his wife left as members. They had excommunicated everybody else. A man was talking to Mary, the wife, who was left. "Well," he said, "I guess you have gotten to the point where your church is pure now." "Indeed, it is!" she said. "Except I'm not so sure about John!" Isn't that always the end of this absurd argument? Who is pure? Who can be pure? Who can ever meet the ideal standards?

As Jesus said in another parable. "Let the wheat and the tares grow together." If you try to remove the tares — the evil — you will destroy the good. The other day, I was working in the yard trying to remove some of the weeds which had grown up in the flower beds. As I pulled up some of the weeds, I discovered that there were some places I could not pull out the weeds without destroying the flower plants. Jesus has reminded us that we sometimes have to let the good grow together with the bad.

God Alone Can Judge

Who is qualified to make the judgment on the nature of another person's faith or religious beliefs? Who has the right or insights to declare that his or her understanding of the faith is the way of knowing what God is like? When we understand the nature of the church from the parable of the dragnet and the tares and wheat, it ought to make us more tolerant toward one another. No person should assume that he or she has the "perfect" insight into theology, the Bible, the church, or the Christian life. No one can presume to speak for God. We never wear God's "glasses," and, therefore, cannot presume to speak authoritatively for God.

The historian, Will Durant, in his volume, *The Reformation*, warned us about those who would use unrelenting fanaticism in judging the beliefs of others. His words raise a huge warning flag.

> Both the Inquisition and witch-burning were expressions of an age afflicted with homicidal certainty in theology as the patriotic massacres of our era may be due in part to homicidal certainty in ethnic or political theory. We must try to understand such movements in terms of their time. But they seem to us now the most unforgivable of historic crimes. A supreme and unchallengeable faith is a deadly enemy to the human mind.[39]

Too often men and women have stood up and declared with absolute certainty what they think are the "answers" to religious inquiry, and then they have judged everybody else as heretics when they did not agree with them. This is one of the tragedies within many denominations today. Some few feel like they alone understand religious truth and others have to believe what they say it is. They have not heard Jesus' warning that the church will always have a mixture in it. Who are we to sit in absolute judgment on another person's theology and declare that this individual is a heretic, because he or she doesn't agree with us? What a claim of divine insight!

Emil Brunner, the Swiss theologian, has warned us against making these judgments. "What then is the real meaning of these words: 'Let both grow together until the harvest?' (He is writing about the parable of the tares and wheat). Jesus forbids us to hinder by force the existence and the work of the evil one. All coercive means are ruled out in the community of Christ. Faith and force are mutually exclusive."[40] Brunner continues his argument with a strong warning:

---

39 Will Durant, *The Reformation* (New York: Simon & Schuster, 1957), 215.
40 Emil Brunner, *Sowing and Reaping* (Richmond, Virginia: John Knox Press, 1964), 73.

The warning not to root out the weeds has one more implication. We are warned not to presume knowing for sure who belongs to the community of Christ and who does not. Many a man who is firmly convinced of being a Christian, of living in faith and in fellowship with God, is in fact quite unconverted. Others who seem to be far from Christ are in reality very near him. Let us beware of judging! God alone knows our hearts. He alone knows whether your zeal for him is holy or unholy, whether the silence and hesitation of your neighbor is really unbelief and indifference against the gospel.[41]

Be careful how you judge other people. Our Lord himself has warned us, "Judge not lest you be judged" (Matthew 7:1). It is easy to presume that we understand what is in another person's mind or heart. But our knowledge is always flawed with partial truth.

God's Final Judgment

This brings me to the final note about this parable. The parable of the net directs us to look ahead to God's final judgment. The net of God's judgment is continuously drawing people into it. There is a present aspect of judgment. We are pulled into his net now. There is a present squirming within the net of God's judgment, but the parable points to the future. Notice the words "sat down." This indicates deliberate, quiet action. Just as a fisherman decides what to keep or reject in his fishing net, God's judgment is certain. There will be a final judgment when God notes those who are a part of his kingdom. That judgment is certain and sure. And you and I cannot presume to know who these people are with absolute certainty.

Remember, this parable is about the kingdom of heaven — those within the church "at large." Church membership is no guarantee that you are in the kingdom of God. Just because a person has his or her name on a church roll does not mean that those individuals are necessarily committed to God or are a part

---

41 Ibid., 74.

of God's kingdom. The thirteenth chapter of Matthew begins with a series of parables where Jesus tells us about the acceptance or rejection of God's word by the souls of men and women, and it ends with a parable about the acceptance or rejection of men and women's souls. This reminds us that Jesus calls us to commitment. We leave judgment to God. Our concern is that we get our own lives right with God. When I speak about God's final judgment, that does not imply that this judgment will be wrathful or vindictive. I believe that God's judgment will be remedial and restorative.[42] I agree with Richard Rohr when he stated: "I do not believe there is any wrath in God whatever — it's theologically impossible when God is Trinity."[43] We will begin in the next chapter of our life after death where we leave off spiritually in this life.

Hear afresh this parable from Matthew: "Again the kingdom of heaven is like a net let down into the sea, where fish of every kind were caught in it. When it was full, it was dragged ashore. Then the men sat down and collected the good fish into pails and threw the worthless away. That is how it will be at the end of time. The angels will go forth, and they will separate the wicked from the good, and throw them into the blazing furnace, the place of wailing and grinding of teeth." Where are you and I in our commitment to Christ?

---

[42] For a further discussion on God's judgment, see my book, William Powell Tuck, *The Journey to the Undiscovered Country: What's Beyond Death?* (Gonzales, FL: Energion Publications, 2012), 27-36.

[43] Richard Rohr with Mike Morrell, *The Divine Dance: The Trinity and Your Transformation* (New Kensington, PA: Whitaker House, 2016), 140.

www.ingramcontent.com/pod-product-compliance
Lightning Source LLC
Chambersburg PA
CBHW030139170426
43199CB00008B/134